10-1

at

Half Time

by

Tony Elliott

DEDICATION

In memory of friends and Spurs fans who left the field too early, in particular for the following who left a positive legacy for all:

Grant Pollard

Joe Inzani

Chris Larkins

Paul Sexton

Thank you!

10-1 at Half Time by Tony Elliott.

This book is a memoir. Memories are imperfect but the stories shared are the author's present recollections of experiences over time. Some names of characters have been omitted, some events have been compressed, and some dialogue has been recreated. Neither the author nor the publisher assumes any responsibility or liability whatsoever on behalf of the reader of this material. Any perceived slight of any individual or organisation is unintentional and the author has endeavoured to tell a truthful story.

Published: January 2021
by
Budding Authors Assistant
www.help2publish.co.uk

ISBN: 9798695280548

FORWARD

Football fans are a strange breed. Away from football, all other aspects of their lives are subject to scrutiny, and possible change, marriage–faith–patriotism–politics–morals all could be discarded in time. But your loyalty to your football team remains forever. It may wain in the dark shadows of failure, but a good result or exciting signing or a great cup run is all that is needed to revitalise the spirits.

Football supporters are not born with a 'chosen team' implant, but at an early age, they make that vital decision on which team they will favour. Some are influenced by their family bonds or place of birth. Some by their peers or simply a fascination with the club's name. Maybe a certain player excites their imagination or could it be the club colours or their history of success. But, one fact is for sure, they will not transfer their allegiances elsewhere.

A vital decision as it shapes life for some forever, will it result in happiness and excitement, glory days and triumph or frustration, humiliation and failure.

The truth is all these feelings will be experienced at some time by the vast majority of fans, and looking back, I am so pleased that my selection has given me so much . . .

COME ON YOU SPURS!

CONTENTS

CHAPTER 1

FOOTBALL FEVER

Hi, my name is Tony Elliott, the title of my memoir is *10-1 at Half Time* and may be of particular interest to any Spurs supporters or anyone brought up in the area of north London where I was living. I was born in 1948, and I am focusing on the period of the late '50s.

I think I was probably typical of a north London lad in the area of Kentish Town, North West London. A normal day for me would be going to school, leaving home for school about a quarter to eight. The street I lived in was called Rochford Street, NW5, London. Fortunately for me, my school was only a couple of hundred yards down the road, sharp left and there I was at St Dominics Primary School at the age of ten. Now people nowadays may not understand this, but the gates were locked, and I and several others would actually climb in over the school gates so we could play football in an almost deserted playground. And this we did for the next hour or so before lessons were called. We were all football-mad; we played football in school, we played football in the park, and we played football in our street. Now our street was again a typical street in those days, virtually very few vehicles apart from the occasional dust cart or rag and bone man. It was simply a matter of putting your jumpers down for a goal and playing until a car appeared or a dog fouled in the street.

Now one of my best buddies was Terry O'Leary and was in my class at St Dominic's. We both had a little job actually in school, which would be frowned upon today by any health authority. We were officially the sick monitors; we were in the fourth year of the Primary school, and in those days free milk was readily available. We had quite a high population and percentage of pupils who depended on their milk in the morning. It would result in, quite often, people overindulging in milk and feeling sick during the day as well as actually being sick. So a message went out for the sick monitors—we were in class 4a. We were called out and released from lessons; we were dispatched to the storeroom where we got our appliances, which were a broom, shovel and bucket of sawdust; and we went to work clearing up the sick. Now for us, it was a coveted job, because once we had despatched the sick and the tools in the correct departments, really, we were free then to roam around a deserted playground. Teachers wouldn't ask how long it took and would just be thankful there were two lads eager enough to do that job.

Now, Terry was a great Spurs supporter and to be honest up to the age of about ten, eleven, and whilst I was football mad, read the papers and watched the Cup Final—which was the only live televised match apart from the internationals at Wembley—I didn't really have a team of my own. The radio would be on throughout the morning in our house and the television in the afternoon, and my father with his pool coupons would be anxiously looking for the results. I hadn't taken a lot of notice in the past, but now all of a sudden, I did take notice. Spurs were playing at White Hart Lane, they were in the First Division and were in the process of rebuilding their team. They had a fair amount of finance available to purchase some of the top players at the time, and I took an interest. And once as a lad, you take an interest, that builds and builds, and you read the papers. My dad's papers were the *Daily Mirror* during the week, the weekends would be *The People* and the *News Of The World*, which was typical of the working class. So, I became a Spurs supporter. There were many in my class, and amongst friends as well, who were Manchester United supporters. Because this was in the era of the 'Munich air crash', even the most neutral supporters suddenly took a liking to United. But by then, I was fixed on the only team for me, the 'Lily Whites' playing at White Hart Lane. I could follow their progress through the papers and, although fuzzy photographs really didn't show you what the players looked like, it didn't matter as I was more interested in the results.

One of my pals at school, Robert Sheed, he was a Spurs supporter, as was his father. And they gave me the opportunity in February 1960 to go and watch one of the most famous matches in football history. Not only was it one of the most famous matches in football history, but it was also my first match and also one of the first times that I travelled in a car. His father, from Kilburn, was a market trader and he had a car, which was almost unknown. So that particular evening when the match was played, it was my first match; it would go down in history as one of the highest-scoring matches; and not only was I travelling in a car but travelling in a car to White Hart Lane. Life could hardly have been better.

But before we carry on with the exploits, the excitement and the results of that glorious evening let me just talk to you more about the environment and life in the late '50s in north London. Obviously, London was in some ways still recovering from the war efforts. There were bombed out places where we played as kids, especially on Guy Fawkes night when all the street would turn out with their assorted fireworks earned by 'Guying'. Our spot was outside Camden Town Tube Station with our Guy pleading 'Penny for the Guy'. Then on 5th November, we'd go to the local bomb site, build a bonfire and create havoc until the Fire Brigade arrived.

Chapter 2

King of the Street

As a child and young teenager, I wasn't aware of a lot of crime. In later years I discovered that some of the guys who'd grown-up on my particular road had served time in prison for various offences which included attempted murder; and a popular crime that was called 'blagging' or 'going across the pavement', where guys, and young guys in particular, would hold up banks and commit various robberies. Now I don't want to give the wrong impression that it was all crime and more crime as we had a great neighbourhood, great street, all the kids played together, and we went out as a street.

One of the great attractions back in my day was Saturday morning's cinema. Where we lived in Kentish Town, we were not far away from what is now a famous music venue, called the Forum. In those days it was a cinema, a very large cinema. Kids in the whole street would go, including my older brother, sister and various friends, probably about twelve of us ranging in age probably between nine, ten to twelve or thirteen.

One of the oldest guys that went with us was a guy called Reginald King, Reggie King. They lived next door to a scrap yard which was at the bottom of the street. Now Reggie was a great guy to go with. He was closer to my sister's age, and he was quite liked by all the girls. Reggie had a great voice and in those days on Saturday at the cinema, there was a talent contest. You'd go out there, and there were up to six acts, and if you were deemed to be very good, you would get ice-cream and various other goodies. But also with those with that flair for drama and singing, it was an opportunity to showcase your talents, and Reggie was excellent. At the age of twelve, thirteen he was singing popular pop songs of the day, mimicking people like Tommy Steele and Cliff Richards. And Reggie turned out to become one of the flagship singers of the '60s, he was Reggie King, Google it and you'll see he was up with the top without ever actually having an outstanding hit. He'd cut several LPs with a band and quoted by Paul Weller as one of his childhood heroes. Reggie was a particular hero if I can use that word, to the Mod generation. He was performing once in Portsmouth and was carried by his Mod fans from the station to his hotel, he was certainly Reggie King of the Mods and one of the most famous singers never to have a hit. So we had various occupational exploits in our road from crooks to top stars.

I remember Reggie as well because they lived next door to a Scrap Yard. Obviously, their house did suffer from an overdose of vermin, including rats. But the Scrap Yard was a great place for us to go as kids because at weekends or in the holidays we could take out a pram, two to a pram, so we'd probably take out four to five prams, and not far from us was a leafy area, an affluent area of

Hampstead. We would head for the heights of Hampstead knocking on doors collecting newspapers in particular. It was great, we'd get a pram load of newspapers, take out the comics put in there as well. If there was a possibility there was nobody in we'd jump over the fence and do a bit of scrumping. It was good fun, nothing nasty, scrumping obviously was the nearest we got to doing anything that could be called illegal. But people generally gave us newspapers, comics, and books. We'd separate the comics as I've mentioned, and any American comics or Dan Dare comics would stay with us, the rest would be weighed in, and we'd receive payment. The average pay for a morning's work, I guess would be in the region of, with two to a pram, maybe we'd get two or three shillings each. Two to three shillings was enough to get you into the cinema, and also get an ice-cream. We didn't really need a lot of money for transport, all cinemas were within a mile radius of where we lived. There were six or seven really good cinemas we could go to, so life was good. We would also often bunk in the cinemas' fire exit, let our street pals in, and then carefully search for empty seats to occupy.

REG KING OBITUARY

Accomplished soul singer and frontman of mod band the Action

REG KING (CENTRE) WITH THE ACTION ON THE COVER OF THEIR ALBUM "ACTION PACKED"

According to Pat Long writing for *The Guardian* about Reg King who had died from cancer aged 65, Reg King "was one of the most accomplished white British soul singers of the 1960s". Long continues to describe Reg who fronted his band the Action, as "the equal of Steve Marriott, Steve Winwood or Rod Stewart, with a voice that was smooth, unhurried and deeply soulful."

According to Long, "The Action were the mods' band of choice: less pop than their contemporaries the Who and the Small Faces, with a repertoire that included versions of the latest soul singles imported from America. Part of their appeal lay in the fact that they remained underground: despite boasting a devoted live following, and being feted by the Beatles producer George Martin, the band never charted and remained largely unknown until the mod revivals of the 1980s and 90s.

King was born in Paddington, west London. His father died when Reg was young and he was brought up by his mother and older sister in Kentish Town, north London. His first experience of singing in public was at Saturday morning children's talent shows at a local cinema."

EXTRACT FROM *THE GUARDIAN* ONLINE, 7th NOV 2010, PAT LONG

CHAPTER 3

CALL OF THE WILD

At home, life was good for me. My dad worked for a tyre company called Pirelli, my mother worked in a market in Kentish Town, a well-known market, still going now called Queen's Crescent Market off the famous Malden Road. She was manageress of Perkins, Dyes and Cleaners. So at a young age, I often used to go there with a pal of mine, Terry O'Leary, Saturday morning after going to Woolworths which I must admit was a Mecca for anybody who felt they could get some soldiers or sweets free of charge. It had a side door which conveniently opened both ways. We would have the initiation of anybody new to our little clique, and that would be Woolworths' as many toy soldiers as you could get by that side door. Not to be admired and not to be encouraged, but it was part of growing up in the '50s.

The great thing about where my mother worked was the area being a market. We had greengrocers, butchers, fruit stalls and as a young lad, ten and eleven, I would walk down there, see my mum and get some money for an ice-cream and just listen to the market traders, just listen to their spiel, their expressions. And that helped me in later life when I was a salesman for a large company, and a sales manager, which I'll discuss later. But, life was really about comradeship, the closeness of family, friends in the street doing things together. You could walk to most places, occasionally we'd get on a bus and commandeer the top flight, windows open, shouting from the windows. We could go to the museums in London, we could go to the Zoo, we could go to various places of interest, but most importantly we could play football as Hampstead Heath was nearby.

Family life was also very important to me growing up, and I was fortunate in as much as we had quite a stable family life. My brother was two years older than me, Peter Elliot, and my sister Betty, Elizabeth Elliot, was three years older. Before we moved to Rochford Street, we lived in rented accommodation in Gloucester Avenue whilst my father, in common with many ex-servicemen, waited on the housing list for a council property then regarded as the 'Jewel in the Crown'.

Gloucester Avenue, NW3, is now regarded as a very opulent and expensive area, famous for the 'Primrose Hill set' but for us children, its fame and glory was its close proximity to London Zoo.

That had a significant impact on my brother Peter and also affected a love for the Zoo by my sister and me. As youngsters, and I'd have been about four or five, we regularly went to the turnstiles of London Zoo, and we were young enough and small enough to get through the bottom of the turnstiles without paying. So that was obviously a very popular location and venue for us to visit. It was amazing, once through that turnstile you'd suddenly come out, and you were very close to the Lions' House, not only could you see lions in their full glory, but elephants too. It was a completely different world bearing in mind documentaries that we see now were not so readily available. To be actually in the vicinity, we could witness animals, wild animals, hippos, rhinos, as well as venture into the Reptile House. My brother from a very early age, fifteen, actually worked in the London Zoo and continued to work in a zoo all his life, from London to America and then to Canada, where until his death, he worked in Winnipeg Zoo. So he was a Zoo man, well respected Zoo man. His original boss was David Attenborough, and his very close friend was a guy called Terry Nutkins, whose future occupation was his own television series, *Animal Magic* with Johnny Morris on BBC1. I worked in the Zoo as well, but only as a student, and that was on the catering side. We eventually moved from Gloucester Avenue to Rochford Street, and it was a happy, happy experience.

My brother Peter was not into soccer or sport in general, he had one obsession, and that was wildlife. He felt completely at home as a Zookeeper in the most famous Zoo in the world, and all his friends were Zookeepers. I previously mentioned his best pal Terry Nutkins with whom he spent most of his free time. I would often see Terry, he was an amazing character and great fun to be with. Like Peter as a youngster, he lived close to the Zoo and worked as a Keeper at an early age. Gavin Maxwell author of *The Ring of Bright Water* became his legal

11

guardian when he was eleven, and it was then that he lost his finger to an Otter. Terry became a household name, working with Johnny Morris on *Animal Magic*, and then with Chris Packham and Michaela Strachan on *The Really Wild Show*. Peter and Terry would drink at the Magdala Tavern in Hampstead, where in 1955 Ruth Ellis shot her lover David Blakely to become the last woman to be hanged in the United Kingdom.

TERRY NUTKINS OBITUARY

Peter's close friend

John Plunkett writing for *The Guardian* describes Terry, who had been diagnosed with leukaemia, as a broadcaster and wildlife expert, "who was familiar to millions of TV viewers as a presenter on *Animal Magic* and *The Really Wild Show*." He goes on to say that Terry had "spent seven years as one of Johnny Morris's co-presenters on teatime children's favourite *Animal Magic*, which ran on BBC1 from 1962 to 1983."

Plunkett also says "When *Animal Magic* ended, Nutkins became one of the founding co-presenters of *The Really Wild Show*, along with *Springwatch* presenter Chris Packham, staying with the show from 1986 until 1993. It remained on Children's BBC until 2006."

EXTRACT FROM *THE GUARDIAN* ONLINE, 7th SEP 2012, JOHN PLUNKETT

CHAPTER 4

FAMILY ROOTS

My father was on the strict side, and my mother was the complete reverse. I often tell people that I can never remember my mother, Josephine Elliott, ever telling me off, she just wouldn't do it. Their backgrounds were completely different, and it's worth mentioning as we're talking about that time in the UK, my mother had quite a varied and strange background. Her father was born in Alexandria in Egypt. He wasn't Egyptian, his parents were Maltese, and his great grandfather was Italian, who'd actually fled Italy after committing a murder and went to the nearest island, which was Malta. And from Malta, the family, with British passports as Malta was part of the Commonwealth, then went to work.

My grandfather, who was a builder and architect, went to Egypt, Alexandria, and had a very successful career there building for the Royal Air Force and also had close ties with King Farouk. But they were proud of their British passports despite their Italian surname of Piacentini. Now my father had volunteered early, he was an Eastend guy from Hoxton. Both Mum and Dad were from large families, he was one of six children from the East End. He volunteered to join the Palestine Police, and at the outbreak of war, was transferred to the North African Regiment.

Their lifestyles were completely different. My mother was from a good catholic convent upbringing. They lived in a certain amount of luxury in Egypt with a townhouse in Cairo and also a villa on the coast in Alexandria. They spoke in Italian and French and also understood Arabic, and obviously, English as well. She was one of six who all eventually came to live in England apart from her elder sister Lucy, who with her husband and two children settled in his homeland of Italy. My grandfather, Pietro Piacentini, followed my mother and her brothers to England in 1949 and settled in Islington. Because of his association with King Farouk, he was a local celebrity and featured in the local *Gazette*.

It was a good life for them if not for the local Arabs. They had a nice car, maids, a cook and it was a good life. My father had the opposite really, he had a bully of a father, who really was not only a bully to the children but also known locally as Nosher Elliott, and most of his time was spent in the pub. His mother was of French extraction, and her father was an onion seller who used to come over from France with his bike and sell onions and garlic around the Eastend. Due to the cosmopolitan population garlic and onions were very popular. But life wasn't very good due mainly to the extreme moods of my grandfather. He didn't really talk a lot, my dad, about the exploits of the war apart from meeting my mum and his life as a youngster. Reading between the lines, I think his childhood was quite abusive, and he was very pleased to get out of the house and serve abroad.

Unfortunately, my father's upbringing and quality of life in his early years certainly proved to have a detrimental impact on his character, particularly in the treatment of my older brother and sister due to his sense of discipline and mood changes.

I mentioned earlier that family life was good, and it certainly was for me, but as I learnt in later years not so for my sister Betty and brother Peter, who both left home as soon as possible. I guess being the youngest and always sympathetic to my father's wishes, I was spoilt, unlike my siblings.

PIETRO PIACENTINI

Betty, Peter and Tony's Maternal Grandfather

Have three wives and a harem, said the Ameer

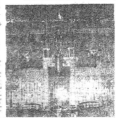

Highbury resident Mr. Pietro Piacentini displays a picture of some of the redecorating work he did on ...

Islington boasts a cosmopolitan population. Apart from the Cockney "natives", many residents can trace their family trees to roots all over the world.

But few of them we dare say, can claim they have been in the company of kings and princes in far-off lands.

Such a man, living in Islington is 74-year-old Mr. Pietro Piacentini, who came to England in 1949 and settled down in Balfour Road.

Mr. Piacentini (despite his Italian sounding name) is Maltese, educated in a French school there and became a building contractor for the Egyptian Government and the British Armed Forces.

Starting with an English company, Mr. Piacentini's first "royal" job was early in 1914, when he went to Turkey with the Kedive Abbas to build a palace on property the king owned in De La Man. But war broke out and he returned to his wife and family in Cairo.

He left the English company in 1928 and went into business for himself. He had built up such a reputation for managing local labour that he was entered on the Egyptian Government contractors list.

One of his biggest jobs was redecorating the 200-year-old Abdin Palace in Cairo for the late King Fuad-father of ex-King Farouk.

EXTRACT FROM ARTICLE THAT APPEARED IN *THE ISLINGTON GAZETTE*, 5TH OCT 1962

17

Chapter 5

Mum's the Word

So a good environment, good parents who tried their best in difficult times to take care. My mum was the outstanding feature of my childhood. She had her own spaghetti making machine, she was a very attractive lady. I was the envy of my friends in as far as we had pasta, ravioli, gnocchi and pizza before you could even buy the ingredients in the UK. And my mother stuck out because we lived in Camden Town/Kentish Town and in those days it was very much a predominantly Irish community, Greek Cypriot and English, and Italian but dominated by the Catholic Churches.

Dominated in particular, by the church attached to my school, St Dominic's Catholic Church, which is a very large church that we went to as a family, excluding my dad, who was Church of England. But it was an influence on the school and in our upbringing.

So my pals' backgrounds I'd say in the main were second-generation Irish, Greek Cypriot a few Italians and a few English. It was very, very mixed, as the whole of that area was in those days, but as a country as a whole, it wasn't so. I remember in the '50s if you saw a black man it would usually be an African. The exodus from the West Indies hadn't really got underway, not in our part of

London, probably had more so in Paddington and Kensington. I remember that if you did see a black face, you'd have to run up, touch him and quickly run away. As I said, they were mainly Africans, in good, bright attire, and there was no racial conflict as far as I knew. Still, in all honesty, my father's generation would look down on them and treat them as being inferior. But it doesn't mean they were racists, simply people of their time, and you know, things have changed for the good, and people realise you don't judge people by the colour of their skin, but probably more so by the football team they support.

So it was a colourful life, it was a cosmopolitan life. Good friends, all working class, we all had that in common. I never knew apart from the one previously mentioned, Robert Sheed, anybody whose dad had a car, certainly, no females had a car. I didn't know anybody who owned their own home, it was seen as being an excellent situation if you actually had a council place. You'd knock for your friends, and the first thing their mums would say to you was "oh have you got a council place or do you rent?".

It was a big thing, probably like comparing owning your own house to renting. So you were proud to have a council place, and your parents were pleased to live in that environment as well. Most of my friends' mothers worked, some of them had two jobs. The friend I mentioned, Terry O'Leary, who had a big impact on my early days, particularly because of the Spurs situation, and where he lived next to the market, unfortunately, lost his dad at nine or ten. It was a very sad day. They used to go to Canvey Island for their holidays. He had a heart attack crossing the bridge to Canvey, and his mother really had it tough. She had Terry and his younger sister to care for, and benefits were not what they are today. I'll always remember the things we took for granted like hot meals and holidays; unfortunately, I didn't realise at the time, but it must have been tough for him, in a one-bedroom room house near the market. His mum had many jobs, cleaning, cooking, and she was a great example of what you could achieve.

Generally, though, people ate enough, played enough, and were fairly happy in their own environment. But Spurs to me was major, but you have to once again remember that we didn't have television coverage of football. I've mentioned that the Cup Final was live, as was England playing at Wembley mid-week, and if you could get away from school, you could see it live on BBC. My father used to conveniently give me a dentist appointment note to take to school so I could come back. He'd be home, I don't know how he managed it, but he'd be home as well to watch the live England Internationals.

CHAPTER 6

GOALS GALORE

But Spurs was the team for me, Tottenham. And again I was lucky that when my dad worked for Pirelli they had a driver there, Jerry, an Irish lad, lived in an old castle near Queen's Crescent. Jerry was in his late teenage years, I'd guess eighteen, nineteen and on his rounds was Cheshunt, and Cheshunt was where Spurs training ground was situated, and he was a mad Spurs fan as well.

Then you could just turn up at the training ground and watch the players train, and when they'd finish get their autographs. When I was on holiday, if he was doing that route, he would tell my dad, and I'd go with him for the day.

Mum would make sandwiches, I'd sit in there with him driving, help him unload the tyres, and have our lunch at Cheshunt. And he'd walk up to the players, I mean, people like famous legend player Danny Blanchflower, and just say "Hi Danny, can you sign so-in-so" and they'd sign it, there wouldn't be any problems you just see him kicking around. For me, that was brilliant and really increased my love for the team, the players were friends of the Fans!

So that fateful day, in 1960, February. One's got to remember that the Cup Final was vital, and this cup match I was going to see was a replay, the Cup Final was the

Mecca, that was the prize. Most fans and players given the choice of being League Champions or winning the FA Cup, the FA Cup was the diamond. The whole day, the Saturday of the FA Cup was devoted to the Cup Final. 8.30 it'd be breakfast with the players, not the pomposity you see now. It was just a great day, it was probably the biggest sporting day of the calendar, followed only by, I would guess, by the Grand National, Wimbledon and Test Matches, but that was the big thing, the Cup Final. The Papers' headline would be 'Cup Final Day', there'd be supplements and for your team to actually be in the Cup Final was massive. It would be the only time you could actually see them live unless you were fortunate enough to be season ticket supporters. For us of that generation, it was the most important day of the year.

So let's go back to that big day. Spurs, 1960, Bill Nicholson, the Manager. He took over in 1958, he played for Spurs as a fullback, took his coaching badges, and when called for by the club, became Manager. His first match went down in history at Spurs. It was against Everton at home and Spurs won 10-4, and that was an amazing score line. He was very shrewd in the transfer market and responsible for bringing in some great players: John White; Dave Mackay; Danny Blanchflower, who'd been signed by the previous manager but prospered under Bill Nicholson; Bobby Smith, legends in their own lifetime. Dave Mackay, Captain of Scotland, one of the greatest half-backs in football; 5' 8", broad-shouldered, born leader; attacking, defending, heading, he had every attribute; he was like a pocket-size version of Duncan Edwards. Danny Blanchflower, Captain of Ireland, what can you say about Danny Blanchflower – a character, had his own newspaper column and the first person to say no to Eamon Andrews on *This is Your Life* after Spurs had won the Double in 1961. He was a wit, he was a shrewd tactician, he was a great captain, and had the gift of the gab like nobody else. Cliff Jones, bought from Swansea for a record amount; fast-footed, could leap like a salmon; was rated the best outside forward in the world at one time, yet would not leave his beloved Spurs. We had a great team.

We had players at their peak coming through, mainly players were brought into the Club, but we also had some good players who came through the Club. The burly centre-forward, called Bobby Smith, played for England, ex Chelsea. Also, we had the famous Clive Allen's father, Les Allen, who was also from Chelsea. Les never played for the England first team, but was a regular goal scorer for Chelsea and Spurs and in my first game he scored 5 goals, and in the following season scored 30!. And in a particular match, my first match, noted as he scored five goals in that game. Anyway, it was a great Spurs team. They were many people's favourite to win the League that season, which they obviously did in 1961, and also tipped as a great bet for the FA Cup. And in their second game, they faced a fourth division team, Crewe Alexandria at Crewe. The score was 2-2, and to be honest, Spurs were just holding their own, they were close to being knocked out of the Cup Final by a fourth division team, as the replay approached many Spurs fans were nervous!

3rd February 1960 Spurs were due to play Crewe Alexandria at White Hart Lane on that Wednesday evening. The anticipated crowd of 65,000 to see Spurs progress from the fifth round of the most famous competition, the FA Cup.

Despite the fact it is 60 years since I witnessed that game, it still lives vividly in my memory. I can remember the evening, my friend Robert and his dad. In those days traffic was very light, probably took half an hour or less. It was an amazing feeling to know you were going to see your team play. Robert and his dad turned up, pleasantries with my mum and dad, and off we roar, driving to the Mecca as far as I was concerned of football, White Hart Lane. As we approached the stadium, down the Seven Sisters Road, we sensed the atmosphere. The people there, the fans chanting, waving their banners, waving their rattles, shop fronts with 'Spurs Will Do It' in the window.

You've got to remember this was a big occasion. If we could beat Crewe, as we should've beaten Crewe, we would be through to the sixth round of the FA Cup. We hadn't won the FA Cup since 1921, forty years before. Anyway, the excitement was building, you felt it. You felt the throb, you felt the feeling, the sense of anticipation, the chatting, the buzz. The Police were on their horses, it was the first time I'd seen mounted Police, and we made our way.

We actually had seats, it was not only my first game but first game with seats, sitting down with the elite. Something I wouldn't replicate until I took my lad to his first football match twenty years later. Anyway, it was tense, it was exciting, the players came out 10 minutes before for a kick around and then went back, and then came out to the familiar tunes that were played at White Hart Lane. Danny Blanchflower led the troops out, and they looked massive in their white outfits, and play commenced to almighty cheers from around the ground. As a young lad of eleven, I'd never been in a crowd like that, never sensed that atmosphere before.

The biggest crowd I guess I've been in was when we'd been on holiday in Ramsgate, on the beach on a hot summer's day, where you couldn't see the sand for bodies, but this was completely different. Mainly male, mainly young male, young men, teenagers, in hats quite a few of them, few females there, the chanting and singing was immense, and Spurs were at it from the start. From the start, they charged, and they scored. It seemed almost every attempt at goal ended up in a score. I lost count of the goals, it seemed amazing to me, used to headlines of 2-0 or 3-1 or 1-1.

Here was Spurs just seeming to ease the goals home, the crowd were crazy in their shouting and cheering and singing and banging and stamping their feet on the seats and on the ground. At half-time, it was the most amazing score, it was 10-1. 10-1 to Spurs, they'd scored 10 goals in the first half, 11 goals in total had been scored, that was a ratio of almost one every four minutes. Can you imagine a scoreline like that today, the news was interrupted, "We're bringing you news from White Hart Lane, amazing score at half-time, 10-1". It was fantastic, it was my first game, and it was the most fantastic feeling, 10-1 at half-time.

They came out in the second half, Spurs probably lacked the desire they'd had in the first. The game ended slightly on an anti-climax really because the crowd were screaming, "we want 20, we want 20", and it had been a record, I think 14 was the record number of goals, and that was in the previous century. But it was a more modest affair in the second half, with Spurs scoring another 3 goals, and Crewe, who never gave up to their credit, scored once.

So it ended 13-2, and people were delirious, it was just a crazy atmosphere. The crowd was at near full capacity, 65,000, and the goal scorers for Spurs were Allen 5, Smith 4, Jones 3, Harmer 1 with gate takings of £8,875. We drove back to Kentish Town in about 30 minutes and deposited me at home. My dad was there, "couldn't believe the score son, just couldn't believe it". I went to bed in a daze and just relived the match time, and experience.

The next day at school, for no reason at all, we were like heroes, we'd been there, we'd witnessed the 13-2. Loads of questions asked, did Les Allen really score 5 goals? Yes, he did. Bobby Smith, I think got a hat-trick, never seen anything like it before, 13 goals, the newspapers were full of it. We two were aloof for that period of time, Arsenal supporters kept away from us, United supporters nodded their head in some sort of satisfaction. We were kings, we were kings of the road, 13-2, what an amazing score, but, 10-1 at half-time. This was not the end of it, this was the beginning of it as far as I was concerned. Obviously, after that, I was a committed Spurs fan, determined to carry on, and I did actually.

TONY'S OFFICIAL PROGRAMME

WEDNESDAY, FEB. 3rd, 1960

COPYRIGHT

VOL. LII. NO. 36

ALL RIGHTS RESERVED

Secretary:
R. S. JARVIS

Team Manager:
W. E. NICHOLSON

Medical Officer:
Dr. A. E. TUGHAN

Chairman:
FRED. J. BEARMAN

Vice-Chairman:
FREDK. WALE

Directors:
F. JOHN BEARMAN, D. H. DEACOCK
S. A. WALE

TOTTENHAM HOTSPUR
FOOTBALL AND ATHLETIC COMPANY LIMITED
Official Programme
AND RECORD OF THE CLUB

CUP REPLAY WITH CREWE ALEXANDRA

THIS evening we give a hearty welcome to Crewe Alexandra on their first-ever visit to our ground in the replay of the Cup-tie played at Crewe last Saturday. Last Saturday's match, played before a record attendance at Gresty Road, contained all the excitement of Cup-tie football, with our opponents twice pulling back after being a goal in arrears, and with a tremendous climax in the last quarter of an hour. We look forward to another exciting Cup-tie to-night, and certainly our players will not under-estimate the ability of the opposition, and while, with the venues reversed, we hope for victory, there is always the uncertainty of Cup-tie football which is the never-failing attractiveness of the competition.

Crewe Alexandra—no one seems to know definitely how the name "Alexandra" came to be adopted, but one theory is that it was taken from the name of a local hostelry—was founded back in the year 1887, and developed as a winter pastime for members of an earlier cricket club. In 1892 they were elected to Division II of the League, and adopted professionalism a year later. Their early years in the League brought them only moderate success, and in 1896 they failed to gain re-election to the League, and remained in non-League football until 1921, when the Third Division (North) was formed. They maintained their status in Division III until 1958, when they were relegated to Division IV.

The present season is only the second occasion that Crewe have reached the Fourth Round of the Cup competition. In the previous 14 seasons they have gone out on nine occasions in the First Round, been dismissed three times in the Second Round, and got as far as the Third once. That was in 1949 when, after defeating Billingham Synthonia 5—0, and Millwall 3—2, both games at Crewe, they were defeated 2—0 at home by Sunderland, then well up in the First Division table.

It was in the season before this that they reached the Fourth Round. On that occasion they defeated South Shields 4—1 in the First Round, Workington 2—1 in the Second, and then defeated Sheffield United 3—1 at Gresty Road in the Third. Two of their goals that day were scored by Bob Finan who had been a member of the Blackpool team that won promotion from Division II in 1936–37 season at the time that Frank Hill, formerly of Arsenal, was skipper of the Bloomfield Road side. Incidentally, Frank Hill was to become Manager of Crewe for four seasons in the early post-war

In the Interests of Ground Conditions, Players on either side will not sign Autographs on the Field

PRICE TWOPENCE

Printed by Thomas Knight & Co. Ltd.,
The Clock House Press, Hoddesdon, Herts.

F.A. CUP, 4TH ROUND REPLAY, FEB, 3RD, 1960

Team Sheet From Tony's Official Programme

On Saturday, February 6th	On Saturday, February 13th
BRISTOL CITY RES.	**LEICESTER CITY**
Football Combination, Div. 1 Kick-off 3 p.m.	Football League, Div. 1 Kick-off 3 p.m.

ROOM FOR 50,000 UNDER COVER

F.A. Cup, 4th Round Replay   Feb. 3rd, 1960   Kick-off 7 p.m.

TOTTENHAM HOTSPUR
White Shirts, Blue Shorts

RIGHT WING				LEFT WING
		GOAL		
		BROWN		
		1		
		BACKS		
	Hills BAKER		HENRY	
	2		3	
		HALF-BACKS		
BLANCHFLOWER (Capt.)		NORMAN		MACKAY
4		5		6
		FORWARDS		
WHITE	HARMER	SMITH, R.	ALLEN	JONES
7	8	9	10	11

Referee: Mr. L. HOWARTH, Yorks.
Linesmen: Mr. F. G. PERKINS, Hants. (Red Flag)
Mr. B. S. SETCHELL, Beds. (Yellow Flag)

11	10	9	8	7
JONES, M.	KEERY	LLEWELLYN	RILEY	COLEMAN
		FORWARDS		
	6	5	4	
	WARHURST	WILLMOTT	JONES, D.	
		HALF-BACKS		
	3		2	
	CAMPBELL		MILLAR	
		BACKS		
		1		
		EVANS		
LEFT WING		GOAL		RIGHT WING

CREWE ALEXANDRA
Red Shirts, White Shorts

ANY ALTERATION WILL BE NOTED ON THE BOARD

F.A. Cup, 4th Round Replay, Feb, 3rd, 1960

CHAPTER 7

DOUBLE CHALLENGE

After that game, driver Jerry, who I mentioned previously from Pirelli's, he used to go regularly with his mates to watch Spurs play on a Saturday afternoon. They were all in their early twenties, late teens, early twenties, and he'd let me tag along quite often. And that was a brilliant ritual going with those lads, listening to their stories and their tales, and just joining in very infrequently, but listening in. We used to go to a Pie and Mash Shop and have pie and mash before the game, it was tremendous.

And it was a strange year for me as well, a momentous year for me, that September of 1960 I started my Secondary school. Roman Catholic school in Kentish Town, Royal College Street, St Richards of Chichester, I was now in Senior school. I failed my 11+, a lot of lads in my class had passed and gone to other schools, but some of my friends progressed through St Richards, and also my brother was there, my sister had left school that previous year.

Not only was it a new beginning for me at school, but it was also a new beginning for me as a Spurs supporter. I was now eleven getting on for twelve, at school, first year and a little aside on that, we had to wear short trousers in the first year, we weren't allowed to wear long trousers.

But, I had the confidence and the trust to make my own way to White Hart Lane. So it would be a regular every other Saturday ritual for me. My mum would make the sandwiches, I'd get a bus to Camden Town, and a bus from Camden Town to Tottenham, walk along Seven Sisters, soak up the atmosphere and then join a queue at the schoolboys' entrance. I'd get there about, I'd guess it'd probably be about half eleven, quarter to twelve. From memory I think the gates opened, for a 3 o'clock kick off, at noon and I'd be there in the front slowly eating my sandwiches, wishing the time away so we could get in there.

And then the gates would open, and there'd be a rush, I'd always make my way to the very very front. They talk about people passing children over in the best possible viewing. I couldn't remember that, but I do remember that adults would make sure kids got to the front. And there you would be at 12 o'clock waiting for three hours just for the team to come out, it was a feeling of excitement, anticipation and that particular year was an amazing year. If I was wonderstruck by that 13-2 score, then a lot more was to come my way for the season '60-61.

I made a habit of going to every home game in the season '60-61, and I kept that up until the end of the season, only missing the home games that were played in the evening. Oh, and what a season it was, Spurs played superb soccer. The Double was spoken of early on by Danny Blanchflower, the Spurs legendary Irish Captain. When he was asked "Danny, do you think it's possible to do the Double?" He said "Yes, I think it is possible, I think we could do it if we have a bit of luck and free of injuries." People scorned and laughed at that because the Double had never been done in this century. It had been done in the previous century, but in those days there were only about ten clubs competing, so it wasn't really like for like.

Clubs had been coming close to the famous Double, Cup and League, some had won the Cup but lost the League, some had won the League but then lost in the Cup Final. So this was a tremendous achievement, and if it could be done, the Double, the holy grail, the impossible dream. Spurs started that season by winning eleven games on the trot: Everton 2-0; Blackpool 3-1; Blackburn 4-1; Manchester United 4-1; Bolton 2-1; Arsenal 3-2; Bolton 3-1; Leicester 2-1; Aston Villa 6-2 and Wolves 4-0, which is a record that has not been surpassed. They were called the Super Spurs, they were called the Invincibles, God knows what the Arsenal supporters called us. Spurs stood out, stood alone, not only in their style of play but by the number of goals they scored and their adventurous outlook on playing football, but it was a good year for me as well.

As I mentioned earlier, it was a year when I started Secondary school, despite my short trousers, I felt I was of age. I was eleven coming on for twelve in the first year of St Richard of Chichester in Kentish Town and had made lots of friends. Unfortunately, lost some of my friends from St Dominics, cos' they'd maybe passed the 11+, or some of them had gone to Havistock, which was a local school on the fringe of Hampstead on Haverstock Hill. Because of its location, it not only inspired local lads to go, but it also had quite a few well-known artists of the day who felt they would be liberal-minded and put their children into a Secondary Modern to mix with working-class children. To the best of my recollection I recall that in my time, Elkan Allan, the famous film producer, his daughter went there, she was the same age as me. And in later days, I understand that John Barnes, a famous footballer, also went to Havistock. More in the present day, the Miliband brothers, the Labour MPs, I believe they too went to Havistock school. It was a real mixture, it had some real toughies in there as well, particularly in my years.

I played in the school football team alongside a friend of mine outside of school, Luigi Salvoni. Now Luigi was an excellent footballer and musician who features later in my story, his parents came over from Italy and lived in Camden Town. Luigi is sitting next to me in the school photo of the under 14s, and directly behind me is the very slight figure of Leonard Whiting who would star, several years on, in the Oscar-winning film *Romeo & Juliet* as Romeo alongside Olivia Hussey in 1968.

St Richard of Chichester School
Football Team 1962

BACK ROW (L-R) SEAN MCGUINESS, IAN GILMORE, PAUL RISEBOROUGH, LEONARD WHITIN,
ALAN BYRNE, RICHARD TWODOWSKI, GEORGE THOROGOOD, PAUL HORGAN, MR RYAN

FRONT ROW (L-R) TATE, MONTGOMERY LONDON, ELLIOT, SALVONI, PATRICK BEADES

35

CHAPTER 8

CHRISTMAS DAY MURDER

On the subject of toughies, I was less aware of say violence, but more of gangs or as we called them in those days, Crews, most areas had their little crew. Whilst I didn't belong to one because of my age, but over this sort of eleven, twelve, thirteen years of age I became aware that there were these specific Gangs, or Crews, in certain areas. Probably where I lived, bearing in mind my mother worked in Queen's Crescent Market, the Queen's Crescent Mob were quite an infamous bunch. They were headed by the most unlikely pair, they were called the Bishop Twins, Teddy and Freddie, and they would have been three or four years older than me. They worked in the market, they were the chicken boys and used to sell chickens from their stall, not live ones I hasten to add.

The twins were identical, frail build with glasses and fair hair always very smartly dressed. They came to my family's attention in the early '60s as they and several of their accomplices had beaten up my brother Peter and his pal David Elvis one evening in the Heath. When my brother regained consciousness, they said they'd mistaken the pair for somebody else, a local lad nicknamed Elvis they offered him a joint and then left.

My sister's boyfriend Ron, who was several years older and a lot tougher, sought revenge on the twins. One had already received 'justice', and the other tried to escape from Ron one Sunday morning. I heard from my brother that Ron, seeing the remaining twin, chased after him into St Dominic's Church, a very large Roman Catholic Church catering mainly for the Irish and Italian Catholics in the neighbourhood with a large entrance at the front and exit at the back. Suddenly there was one of the twins running through the church chased by Ron. My brother walked the streets safely after that.

Their names appeared again several years later for a much more sinister reason due to a notorious murder on Christmas Day in 1964. The Bishop Twins and their associates, after a drinking session in various pubs in the Queens Crescent area on Christmas Eve, decided they would gate crash a party in nearby Chalk Farm. About fifteen of them got into a van and drove to the party. Denied entry they then broke into a Dairy opposite and started throwing bottles and other missiles at the flat where the party was being held.

Dairyman Eirwyn Griffiths, 38 years old, tried to stop the Gang and was beaten up and stabbed. A neighbour, Michael Munnely aged 23, was visiting his mother and brother over Christmas and despite the odds went to the help of the injured Dairyman. Trying to pull his attackers away he was stabbed and was pronounced dead soon after. Michael Munnely was a reporter for *The People* Sunday newspaper, and his violent murder was prominent in the news on Boxing Day both local and national.

I didn't realise until I called on my best pal Willy Steele on Boxing Day morning, who informed me that Freddy Bishop was charged with the murder and twelve other youths were charged with causing an affray. One of whom lived in the same flats as Willy, it was hot news for several days known as either 'Christmas Day Murder' or the 'Dairy Murder'.

Frederick Bishop was found guilty and sentenced to a term of Life Imprisonment. Michael Munnely was later awarded the George Cross for his act of bravery, and the Dairyman survived his life-threatening injuries.

CHRISTMAS DAY MURDER

Chapter 9

Local Crews

There were other Crews in that part of North West London which included Kentish Town, Camden Town and Somers Town. Apart from the Bishops, there were a group of lads from the Archway area known as the Torrano Mob who were particularly notorious. I knew of several but never crossed their paths. Still, several of their members were to achieve notoriety in later years. However, certainly, the toughest and most infamous were known as the Somers Town Crew, and they drank in a pub called the Somers Arms.

Somers Town in the '60s was a rundown area, home to many second-generation Irish, and well known to me for several reasons. Most importantly, the local flea pit called the Tolmer Cinema in Tolmer Square, Somers Town, where irrespective of age you could gain entry. Films were always old 'B' movies, and you ran the risk of catching fleas or being bothered by the numerous men who occupied the back seats with raincoats on their laps. Also, a good friend of mine a Greek Cypriot lad nicknamed Po, as his surname was too long to remember, his father owned a Fish & Chip Shop close to the Pub, and we would hear stories of various incidents including shotguns being fired.

My friends and I were only fourteen or fifteen at the time and were very impressed when the local fair at Hampstead Heath was on. The buses stopped at the Bus Terminus where we would meet, and suddenly the No 24 Bus would stop and out would come a dozen or so young men and several girls and the cry would go up "it's the Somers". We would avoid any eye contact as they dismounted and began their proud walk towards the Heath. Some of my friends had older brothers in the gang, and they rejoiced in the knowledge that they were untouchable. The one name that always stands out in my memory was one of the gang called Chopper Bailey, now was that due to his manhood or the fact he carried a chopper into battle. Unsurprisingly I never did ask!

CHAPTER 10

CHARACTERS

Away from that, there were other characters that I remember from the mid-60s One famous character who my future brother-in-law knew very well indeed. He ran a car lot, second-hand cars, very close to our yard at Queens Crescent. His lot eventually became part of Camden Lock. This guy was called Freddie, and he would have been five years older than me. Very good looking guy, smartly dressed, a real wheeler-dealer in the finest Del'boy style.

There was one story of an incident that sticks in my mind that I heard when I first started working in a company called Elliott Perkins. It occurred about two years before I started, and was folklore at the time. Elliott Perkins was a combination of Perkins and BG Elliott, no relation. Elliott had branches in North West London including the branch at the Camden Lock. Perkins were also a North London city company that had several branches, and both companies merged in the early '60s. Eventually, the Camden Town branch was closed, and it became, in later years, the Lock, the Camden Lock. Anyway, one of the directors sold one of the company lorries to Freddie. As Freddie didn't know the director very well, he asked someone who did know him to say that if any lorries were going, he'd like to buy them. So the director sold one of the lorries thinking he'd done a really good deal. Unfortunately, however, it wasn't up to the standard expected by Freddie, and the message came back to him, "I want my money back, you sold me a wrong' un". Not really used to this type of behaviour, public schoolboy, he said: "Oh, no, give him a message back, it was sold as seen ol' chap and you always take a risk when you buy as seen, and I have no intention of giving you your money back, or taking the vehicle back". A further message came back on the Wednesday that Freddie was coming in with the lorry, parking it, then coming up to see him, and if the cash wasn't forthcoming, he would personally cut one of his ears off.

Alright, now the director got the message. Thinking *uh, how do I deal with this?* he asked the messenger, someone who knew Freddie, "is he serious?", "yes, Gov'nor he's serious". "Oh, well this is a bit difficult, isn't it? I've said no, and I don't like to go back on my word, let me think about it." Anyway, he didn't say anything to anybody. Thursday came and went. Friday, there it comes, you can hear the lorry pulling into the yard, and outstepped, in his sheepskin coat – Freddie– 6ft of aggression. Freddie went in to see him and came out very soon after, quite happy, left the lorry there, and walked to his car lot which was only a five-minute walk away. When asked about what'd happened, the director answered: "well I didn't intend to pay him, but I'd spoken to my wife who said that if I'd lost an ear how would I keep my glasses on, so I decided to pay him".

The other story, which would have been in the later '60s when I was working for the company and based in a branch in Paddington, 6 South Wharf, Paddington. Next door to us there was quite a lot of work going on. There was a warehouse, and a team of guys, ex-university guys typical of the age, long hair, barefoot in many cases, it was the summertime. They used to come into the branch, buy battening and shelving, and they used to store records there, in the warehouse.

I was on the trade counter at the time, which was not like the trade counters you see in a modern shop. I used to make tickets and bills out for the customers. And one of the guys of this team, they used to come in about two or three-handed and just walk the timber back, a very well-spoken guy, long blond hair; open sandals; T-shirt; and flared jeans, said to me "by the way we've been doing quite a lot of business with you on a cash basis, it would be handy if we could open an account, do you know if that's possible?" Me, wanting to score a few brownie points, said "well hold on a second, I'll ring up and speak to our MD".

Then, because we were so small, seven branches, you could speak to Mr David, as he liked to be called. As habit directors were called by their Christian names, but with Mr, whereas the workers were just called by their surnames. So I'd have been Elliott. That was until I got

44

onto the board, I was always just known as and gestured to as Elliott. Anyway, so I thought I'd score some brownie points, the customer was working next door wanting to open an account, so I rang up.

I managed to get straight through, the secretary put me through. "Oh, Mr David I've got a customer here who has spent quite a lot of money with us, they're doing a hell of a lot of work next door in the warehouse and are interested in opening an account." And the voice, I could hear Mr David *um*, I could imagine him leaning back sucking on his pipe, *um*. "Well, Elliott, when one makes a decision as colossal as giving a man credit, I really have a couple of principles worth looking at". So I said quietly, as there were a couple of customers about 10ft away, I said "Yes, Mr David, what do you think?" "Well, for a start Elliott", he said, "and very important, judge a man by his shoes". I said "oh", he said "yes, yes it's never failed me. If he's got black leather shoes, particularly brogues, he's somebody you know is a man of standing. If he's got brown shoes, *um* slightly reckless but still worth considering. If he's got suede shoes, the answer is certainly no. So without giving the game away, what has he got?" I said "oo, well actually, in a very low voice, he's got open sandals." I won't repeat what he said to me, but it was clear that he wasn't giving this particular guy a credit account. So I turned around and looked at the guy and said, "I'm sorry, but it doesn't seem like we're doing accounts today." He just looked at me, smiled, and said "fair enough, we'll go on paying cash". I'm pretty certain he was Richard Branson who had founded Virgin Mail Order in 1970 originally selling records via their warehouse before opening a shop in Oxford Street, London where in 1972 Virgin Records was born.

CHAPTER 11

BUILDING A GREAT TEAM

I am jumping ahead in my tales, let's focus again on Spurs on the most memorable season '60-61, and their quest for the impossible League Championship and FA Cup. Spurs started in some style winning their first eleven matches, a record that still stands today. I was in the fortunate position then of being at school, not working, meaning that apart from the evening matches I could go to all Spurs home games. Which I did, by myself in most cases, normal transport by bus, walking up Seven Sisters Road and then returning, normally, full of happiness and excitement because it was another Spurs victory. Desperate to get hold of the *Pink Standard* which went out on a Saturday and was devoted to Football, Football results, unfortunately no longer in existence, it hasn't been, probably, for the last 40 years.

Anyway, let's get back to Spurs. What a star, Danny Blanchflower's prediction of a Double didn't seem so odd when you look at our stats. It was a great season, all the buzz and excitement walking towards the ground along Seven Sisters Road. Getting there very early, it was as one with the shops, signs out in most shops, 'Come on you Spurs', 'Come on the Lily Whites' and it didn't fail to deliver. If you look back on that golden season at just some statistics that were worth noting, we scored in total

115 league goals; a record season; a record number of points and a record number of victories. And let's go through if we may, the squad of players, cos' in the main it was a standard eleven players who played that season. There was not much call on the reserves, though there were some excellent reserves to be called on if necessary.

In goal, we had Bill Brown, superb goalkeeper, Scottish international, one of the safest pairs of hands in Scottish goalkeeping history, which is probably not too difficult bearing in mind their abysmal record of goalkeepers, Bill Brown, great guy. Two full-backs, both came through the Spurs youth system, Peter Baker, a Hampstead lad and Ron Henry a local lad. And they were responsible for the now common factor of full-backs chasing upfield, getting upfront and putting crosses over. They used to stay in their part of the field and not wander past the halfway line, but their manager, Bill Nicolson, encouraged both Henry and Baker to get up there, get the crosses in. We expected to give some goals away, we'd be happy if we gave two away because we knew we had the resources in midfield and particularly up front to score goals, and Baker and Henry did their bit in achieving that.

Baker was never capped for England, Henry was once by Alf Ramsey; unfortunately, it was a 5-1 thrashing by France, and he never got the chance again. The two centre-backs were Danny Blanchflower, possibly the best-known footballer of that generation. He often appeared on television, tremendous speaker, much in demand by newspapers and advertising agencies. Despite his age, around 34 in that Double year, was seen as a great player and voted 'Player of the Year', he was also captain of his national team Northern Ireland. Alongside Danny, was the gaunt figure of the centre-half Morris Norman, standing at 6ft 2", 'Mr Dependable', who was also a regular for England. Great in the air, and regularly went up-field for corners causing havoc with the oppositions defence and scoring many vital goals in mid-field. In mid-field, the one and only, Dave MacKay. Dave Mackay, 5ft 8", barrel-chested, strong in a tackle, great shot, could dribble – one guy who you could really call a leader - if Blanchflower was the leader, MacKay was second in charge. He never knew when to admit defeat, he was a great guy, very popular with Spurs fans, he also captained Scotland; actually, one of the few players from that team that went on to another club and made even more history. He went in the late '60s, signed by Brian Clough for Derby, who were then in the Second Division. He was Captain and lifted them to the First Division. He took over as manager when Clough left and secured the Division One League Championship with Derby. Great guy, tremendous, one of the greats of the '60s and '70s with his record at Derby County.

Alongside him in mid-field, John White, another Scottish lad, very young, been signed in the previous season. He was still doing National Service, so he didn't play that many games, but in '60-61 he replaced Tommy Harmer our regular inside forward. He then went on to be a Scottish international, and he was a great. I'm trying to compare him to a modern-day player, maybe someone like Paul Scholes from Manchester United. He scored lots of goals, he seemed always to be in the right position, and his passing was 100%, a key member of the team.

And then a player I've mentioned before, on the outside flank, Cliff Jones. Cliff Jones, what a great player, recognised as one of the best in the world. Italian clubs tried to tempt Spurs to sell him with offers over £100,000, which was a world record offer in those days. But Spurs were not inclined to let him go, and I believe Jones was so happy at Spurs he would have stayed despite the fact that his wages were about £12 a week and he could have earned over £100 a week abroad. But he was great, very fast, fleet-footed I think the expression is, great in the air, despite his height, 5ft 7", he could jump like a man of 6ft 2". Great goal scorer for Spurs as well, in that season he scored 18 goals including cup matches. I met him once, at the Old Bailey. I was waiting to give evidence on behalf of the Prosecution for a company. A South London crew were involved in short-term fraud and had hit the company that I worked for. I was sitting there waiting, I knew I wouldn't be on for a while, and who should pass me, Cliff Jones. As he walked past I chased him, and he came back and sat next to me, and we had a chat, he told me about his life, and I told him about my experiences. What surprised me with Cliff Jones though, one, he didn't look any older, in fact, he had more hair because in his playing days it was cut in a sharp crew, but his dress as well, the way he was dressed was reminiscent of the late '50s early '60s. For those who remember the style, he had a suit on. The jacket was an Italian style bum freezer; it had cloth buttons on the jacket and the sleeves; the trousers were a very tight fit with a little split at the bottom of each leg; above the split was another cloth button which was very stylish in the early '60s, and most surprising, he had a pair of winkle pickers on which hadn't seen space since about mid-60s. But a great guy and really admired by all the fans, capped a record number of times by Wales at the time, an outstanding player, world-class as many of the Spurs team were.

And then on the other flank, we had Terry Dyson. Again Dyson, on the short side, I think he was about 5ft 5"-5ft 6", his father was a jockey, and it was thought Dyson would also go into horse riding. But no, his skills lay in soccer, he came through the Spurs youth team. Dynamic, enthusiastic player, vigorous in a tackle, could beat his man, could cross the ball, and again for his height was surprisingly good in the air. And Dyson in that season scored for Spurs 17 goals in league and cup, which was a great return.

Now, next to Terry Dyson in the middle were two dynamic goal scorers, both ex-Chelsea players. Let's start off with the number one, Bobby Smith, signed by Spurs in the '50s, been a regular goal-scorer, top of the charts Tottenham, great character, a Yorkshireman. He was a big lad, broad lad, aggressive, struck fear into the goalkeepers in the days when you could barge the goalkeeper in the air, struck panic into the defenders, took no prisoners despite his size, good on the floor as well as good footwork, as evident when he played for England. An outstanding player for Spurs and England and, in that notable season, Bobby Smith scored a total of 31 goals for Spurs.

Then alongside him was Les Allen, father of Clive, a member of the Allen dynasty who became professional footballers. He was a great goal scorer for Spurs, slightly underrated I believe. When you think in that Double winning team, he scored a total of 27 goals and lost his place in the team early the following season because, the one and only leading goal scorer, probably the greatest striker at that time, Jimmy Greaves, became available.

Greaves had fallen out with his Italian club and, Spurs being Spurs Bill Nicholson was there. He managed to secure the transfer of Jimmy Greaves in season '61-62 at the expense of Les Allen. He still got games, Les, because Bobby Smith was often injured. Still, you can't imagine a player who'd scored that many goals not being your number one striker the following season. I'm trying again to think of another comparison, it would be like Spurs signing Messi and Kane being a sub, it was that big a gulf really. But, in that season Allen and Smith, the four forwards, if you classify Dyson and Jones as forwards as well, in all the games they scored a total of 96 goals between them. That would've been more goals than most, if not all - I haven't got the records, First Division clubs scored in total. Dyson, Jones putting the ball in, Smith and Allen finishing. By the way, Les Allen I said earlier was underrated, he never got an England cap, I think these days with his goal scoring record he'd have been a regular.

CHAPTER 12

WINNING THE LEAGUE

That great Tottenham team just continued with victories, occasional defeats, goal-scoring sprees, often scoring four or more. Talk of the town, an exciting place to be, amazing atmosphere. Brilliant, brilliant for supporters, brilliant for football fans generally, 'could that Double be achieved in their lifetime?' an amazing period. Well Spurs continued, continued as they went on, it was an amazing season for them, after eleven straight wins they actually achieved 31 victories from 42 games. Sixteen away games in victory, 115 goals scored, the list of records broken goes on and on. The title was eventually won on an emotional night at White Hart Lane on April 17th with a 2-1 victory over their nearest challengers, Sheffield Wednesday. Such was their dominance that all their rivals recognised the contest was effectively over long before that night. By the halfway mark in the title race no bookmaker, not that I was a betting guy when I was twelve, would accept money on Spurs.

And it was all done in superb style under the leadership of Bill Nicholson, a member of the great 'push and run' side, the team built on the greatest Tottenham passing game, thrilling spectators wherever they played. How the crowds flocked to see us home and away, the highest attendance ever achieved, over two million in the league and almost half a million in the seven cup games. More fans followed Spurs' games both home and away than ever previously achieved in league and cup games combined, Spurs had caught the imagination of the Sporting Public, could they achieve the 'impossible' League and Cup success, fans of both Spurs and their competition were eager to witness Spurs in action in what would prove to be a historic season. If they could achieve the Double, they would be hailed as the greatest English team ever, and I was fortunate enough to see them in action. The league secured could they do it? Could they win the F.A. Cup?

The first cup game, I was there, January 7th, home to Charlton Athletic, who I believe at the time were in the Second Division. Despite their lower place they put up quite a fight, Spurs eventually won by 3-2, in front of a crowd of 55,000. Goal-scorers, Allen again and little Terry Dyson. Then, would you believe it, who would be drawn against us at home, bearing in mind 10-1 at halftime, yes for the next round we were drawn against Crewe Alexandria at home. There must have been some nervousness on the Crewe team when they came out on the pitch for that game. I was there, expecting, could we achieve double figures once again? No, we didn't, they put up a fight, as you would expect, but it was still an overall victory for Tottenham 5-1.

Dave MacKay was amongst the goal scorers, alongside Jones, Smith, Allen and Dyson, again 55,000 supporters turned up. Now, it's getting serious, the next round was February 5th and Spurs were away to one of the top teams of the time, Aston Villa. Well, we secured victory, with two goals, and we went on in the draw. We were picked out for another away game, to possibly one of the most difficult ties, Sunderland at Roker Park. They had a tremendous record there, a very hard team to beat and one which really would test Spurs even at their best. It was a difficult time for Spurs, but they managed to come away with a 1-1 draw thanks to a goal scored by Jones in front of a gate which exceeded 60,000. So the replay at home against Sunderland, could we do it? Could we reach the last eight? Yes, we could. With a 5-0 victory, with MacKay scoring again, plus Smithy, Allen and Dyson in front of 65,000 supporters.

You bear in mind now that even the modern capacity stadium we've got, the brand new stadium which cost near on a billion pounds, one of the biggest and most extravagant in Europe, its capacity is 65,000, we got that number in the small White Hart Lane ground in 1961. Now, the next game. We were through now to the final four, and the next game was against Burnley, this was the semi-final played at a neutral ground. Now, Burnley was a top team, they'd finished in the top three, they were seen as being, possibly after Spurs, one of the second top teams in the First Division. Their side was packed with internationals, Scotland, Ireland, and England. All the way through their team was class, there was expertise, experience and achievements, Burnley was a top, top club. The semi-final was played at Villa Park, Birmingham, so neither team had a home advantage. Unlike these days when the semi-final is played at Wembley, possibly the London teams, if they're competing have some sort of advantage. But, it was at Villa Park, Birmingham and Spurs came out convincing victors by 3-0, Smithy got two, Jones got one, it meant we were in the final. What an achievement, how exciting, we got the League, could we get the Double?

CHAPTER 13

CUP AND DOUBLE

In the '60s football, whilst it was a major event for most sports fans, it didn't actually grab the headlines, but it did now. Spurs were the talk of the town, could this jinx the Double, that'd played havoc with other teams, including the great Manchester United and Wolverhampton Wanderers. Could Spurs overcome it? Could they be the first modern-day club to get the Double? Well the final was played at Wembley, I didn't go to the final, but I saw it on television, and you can imagine the excitement with it being my team. First time I'd ever seen Spurs play live on a television. And in the street I lived on, in Rochford Street, I put banners outside our door and windows so everyone going past would know this was a Spurs household. And if you walked around London in those days, because bearing in mind Kentish Town, Camden Town are reasonably close to both Arsenal and Tottenham, opinion would be divided in North London between those two clubs. Probably more East London would be West Ham and certainly, North West London, more Spurs I guess, North London Spurs and Arsenal. Anyway, there was a sense of excitement, you could see it, you could feel it. Even on non-match days, fans were loitering around the ground just to get the buzz, the feeling. Going to the training ground at Cheshunt where

I told you I sometimes went with my father's workmate who was a driver for Pirelli and also an avid Spurs fan, the feeling of excitement was so intense as we waited for the Final.

Then the actual day, the Cup Final 1961 Spurs against Leicester. In fairness watching it on the television, Spurs and Bill Nicolson after the game didn't do themselves the credit they deserved to. They didn't play in their normal style, I think the occasion overtook everybody, and unfortunately, Leicester City fairly early on lost one of their key players to injury, and no substitutes were allowed on the day. But, Spurs came out victors, that was the number one objective, and they beat Leicester City 2-0 thanks to goals by Bobby Smith and Terry Dyson. And Bobby Smith himself admitted, and he played a vital role, that he was badly injured prior to the final. He didn't really want to go public on that, he was desperate to play. He had his own personal doctor in Palmers Green, where he lived and the doctor was giving him pain killers to see him through unbeknown necessarily to the club. This is an amazing fact that in the morning of the Cup Final Bobby Smith actually went to Palmers Green to see his doctor who gave him a painkilling injection and then came back to their hotel before the team left for the final. He'd got up early, got to Palmers Green, had his injection, then back down to the hotel. You can imagine these days, how protected the players are. Still, in fairness, they'd have their own private doctor administering whatever medicine was needed.

Anyway, it was a day of triumph, a day of glory, the Double, the amazing Double had been achieved. What a feeling of excitement, what a feeling of pride. I went round my pals, we met up in North London as I said when we were twelve, thirteen, we just paraded around Hampstead and Kentish Town with flags and banners claiming our allegiance to Spurs. One of my pals, Brian O'Sullivan, great lad, good Irish family, friends for many years, we'd gone to junior school together, his mother was from the O'Brien clan, and her brother was the boxer, famous boxer, Danny O'Brien. We put together cardboard on a post showing a drawing of the Spurs cockerel with a message, this was just before the Cup Final, a message 'This Cock will Crow at Wembley', and we were parading it around Hampstead bus terminals. We left it there on the side when we went off for lunch and carried on after until a member of the public stopped us and said, "you should be ashamed of yourselves that's quite obscene". What'd happened, while we were away, I presume was one of the drivers or bus conductors had changed the 'C' to a 'G', so it said 'This Cock will Grow at Wembley', so we hastily put an end to that.

Brian was a good lad, my age, one of those guys who always had to be in the forefront, he was desperate to be a man of his times. We drifted apart probably around fifteen, sixteen years of age. His new best buddy was a guy called Steve Copsey from quite a large family, whose father was a musician. Nice guy, really nice family, one of his older brothers, Derek Copsey author of *Diana Remembered 1961-1997*, married Dennis Healey's daughter, Jennifer Healey, who was a teacher at the school nearby at Gospel Oak. Brian spent a lot of time with Copsey who had more liberal friends, more hippy type friends, and we sort of lost contact. I always remember that one sad morning when I got a phone call. I was then married, I was 22, and I was told that he'd died, he'd died of a drug overdose. I attended his funeral at Stoke Newington. Anyway, let's end that particular season on a bright note. Brian and I, we were there when the Spurs Team Bus paraded down the High Street to go to the Town Hall for a civic reception. Thousands upon thousands of fans there including Brian and I, we were not wavering our 'This Cock will Grow at Wembley', we left that to others. It was a superb day and a fitting end to the season, and ahead of us, we had another exciting season '61-62.

CHAPTER 14

ST PANCRAS CALLS

Let's go away from soccer for a moment. As a family now, I was twelve or thirteen, and we moved away from Rochford Street just around the corner to a flat within a house, 29 Mansfield Road, NW3. Mr Flippin, who was an Irish lad, worked for the local boroughs as a painter. He and his partner had the ground floor, and we had two floors above them, which meant we had three bedrooms so my sister could have her own bedroom, I shared with my brother. We had access to a flat roof through the loft, which was quite nice to sit out on with my dad and with the radio on listening to the cricket. I really enjoyed my time at Mansfield Road. My brother was working full-time by then for the London Zoo, my sister was working full-time as well, and going out with Ron Turner, who ended up being her husband. Ron was a Somers Town lad, as I mentioned early on.

My main interest was still soccer with my pals, and I played for three different teams. I played for a Sunday team called Kilburn Priory, that was managed by a Dustman called Charlie. Unfortunately, without going into the details, some bad things happened, and the team was disbanded. I was also playing for St Pancras under 14s in addition to playing for the under 14s at school where two of our members went onto some fame.

I've already touched upon Luigi Salvoni and his footballing ability and musical skills, but Luigi actually went on to became a professional drummer and producer and was the founder of Upland Records. He also played with the Punk rock band Moon in the mid-'70s and then formed Sniff 'N' the Tears.

I also played for St Pancras, King's Cross and St Pancras under 14s. Each school in those days, in that area of North London, could nominate two players from their school who they thought should go for trials for St Pancras. In our case, St Richard of Chichester, the two people they nominated were Luigi Salvoni and me. We both got into the St Pancras team based on our trials. I did it by default really, but Luigi did it by his skill.

When you went to Parliament Fields, where the trials were, which is just before you get to Hampstead Heath, you put down the name of your school, your age and your position. I got there towards the end, and when I looked through all the names, it was a bit daunting. I used to play centre-forward, and I noticed that there were four or five centre-forwards, so I looked for the right-back position, and there was only one other player who had put his name down as right-back. So I put my name down as right-back, and I got in as right-back.

Playing alongside me at left-back was a really good footballer which you could see at an early age. His name was Tommy Yalden, and he went on to be scouted during a St Pancras match by Arsenal. Arsenal was then managed by the famous Billy Wright, and Tommy signed schoolboy forms with him. I don't think he ever played for the first team. Still, if you Google 'Tommy Yalden' you'll see he had a full career in football, he played for Aldershot for a record number of appearances, and also played in the States as well.

St Pancras Under 14's 1961/62

(1)   Tony Elliott

(2)   Tommy Yalden (Arsenal, Aldershot, Reading)

(3)   Brian O'Sullivan

(4)   Luigi Salvoni (Famous Drummer Sniff N the Tears)

(5)   Terry O'Leary (Best Friend)

Chapter 15

Close Call

So football was very much in my mind most of the time, and we lived in the Gospel Oak area, as I said in Mansfield Road, very close to Parliament Hill Fields. There was a famous Lido at Gospel Oak, and on a Sunday, when I was about thirteen, I often used to leave home on a late afternoon and walk through past the Lido into the main part of Parliament Hill Fields. There'd often be groups of lads playing football there. I'd just stand watching and always be invited to join. I made several friends from just joining in and meeting up again.

On one particular day, which will always stick in my memory, I left home about half-past four, five o'clock, crossed the road, Mansfield Road, turned right then entered the Park area near the Lido. Big area, very large area that as you carried on walking up the path would lead you into Parliament Hill Fields. The area was empty as I was walking, very quiet, and I suddenly heard footsteps near me. As I turned around there was this, to me what appeared to be a giant of a man, I'd probably say he was about 6ft 2". A strange look to him, gummy, very vacant eyes, his trousers were about 3" too short, and he had a pair of hobnail boots on. He walked with me, without me encouraging him, and he started a conversation. "Where you going? What you doing?" "I'm going to watch the football, hopefully, join in."

"Oh, you like it, do ya'?" So that carried on for a couple of steps, and I felt him getting closer and closer. There was nobody else around, we were approaching the Lido area, and suddenly his hand is in my hand. He looked at me with a smile on his face, and we had bushes to the left of us and said to me in an evil tone "come into those bushes, I'm going to show you mine and you're gonna show me yours." I was panic-stricken, to be honest, and as I looked round in desperation, slowly being tugged away, I noticed in the far distance walking in the opposite direction on the other side of that expanse of lawn and grass, there was one solitary figure walking. I could make out it was a guy, probably in his thirties or forties. I looked over, put my hand up and waved at him, as I did so I looked at the guy who was trying to pull me into the bushes and said in a calm voice, "Oh, there's my dad, would you like to see his as well?" And I shouted out "Hi Dad", and I waved again. With that, he let go of my hand, turned around and just ran. I went straight back home, told my dad of the experience and straight away he took me to the nearest Police Station, which was quite a famous one, the Holmes Road Police Station.

They took my dad and me in a car to that area, and looked around, gave them a description, never heard anything else about it. No harm was done to me mentally, and certainly not physically, but it's a memory. I guess a lot of us hit on a certain situation where you need to be fairly quick-witted to get out of it. Up to now, I've never been in that situation again I'm pleased to say, but even the thought now is scary.

CHAPTER 16

SUMMER HOLS

It's now that glorious time of year, summer holiday time. Apart from being off school, playing with your pals, going places as a teen with your friends, cinema, London museums, for us as a family it was our most enjoyable experience. Mum and Dad both worked, worked hard, and between them saved enough money to ensure that once a year as a family of five, we got away for our two weeks' annual holiday which was always in Ramsgate. Mum, particularly, looked forward to a session by the sea since she'd been in England, it was a stark contrast to her life mainly in Alexandria on the Mediterranean in Egypt. Alexandria was the place to be for people, French, Italian, Greek, it was a holiday sort of paradise.

Mum claimed that she woke up in the morning and never saw anything but a blue sky, which was a sharp contrast as she entered England. East End of London, post-war, late '40s was not the best place in the world to live, smog, damp, grey skies. It must have been very difficult for her to adapt. Sharing accommodation in a large house with my father's family, his mother one floor, his sister the second floor, his other sister lived on the third floor and Mum and Dad with my sister and brother on the top floor, in the east end of London, outside toilet, difficult particularly for my mum.

My dad, well he was used to those conditions, he was born in Hoxton, six children, a mother who worked very hard to keep the family going, a father whose life was spent in the Pub or street fighting, could be very cruel and vindictive. My dad's spare time, I think was just walking with his brothers and sisters, the streets of London. Often going to the Salvation Army for hand-outs, for soup etc. So he was pleased when he got away, volunteered for a job in the Palestinian Police and then the Army. To him, holidays were particularly important, it gave him a chance to get away. It was the only chance for the family to get away, to see the sea, that was amazing.

Bearing in mind that people, working-class people didn't have cars, to spend two weeks by the sea in the summer was just unbelievable, it was all we looked forward to for months. My mum would tell us tales of her experience living in Alexandria where her family had a villa and beach hut, and how on Sundays they would go to their beach hut and her mother would make pasta. The beach hut was on two floors, and her father would go up to the top floor for the afternoon, and after a big bowl of pasta would be sleeping, snoring. At the same time, the rest of the family used to sit out protected from the sun. What a life, what a difference.

But Ramsgate was our mecca, loved it, looked forward to it so much. We saw the countryside on the train from Victoria to Ramsgate, we saw cows, which we'd never seen before. I don't know how we got to Victoria, I guess, we didn't have a phone, and we never had a car, so I imagine, we had a bus stop at the bottom of our road so we probably just got a bus to Victoria. I know from Ramsgate Station we got a cab, and that was the only time we travelled in a cab. So we used to go to a regular place, bed and breakfast. I can't remember if we had two rooms, one for the children and one for my mum and dad or whether we all shared one, but it wouldn't have mattered. There were communal baths, bathrooms and toilets and each room had its own basin, hand wash basin, so you could wash if you wanted to in the privacy of your own room. It was brilliant, it seemed to me the sun was always shining, we'd get out early on the beach, by 10 o'clock the beach would be packed solid.

We would go along the cliffs, walk as a family from Ramsgate to Broadstairs, we'd sometimes go to Margate. Two glorious weeks, the only time we ate out as a family all be it pie and chips or fish and chips. Our Boarding House was bed and breakfast and evening meals, so lunchtime was up to us. I can only remember sunshine days.

My brother and sister would go their own little way, and I'd stick with my mum and dad. Ice-creams galore, slot machines, and then in the evenings sometimes there was a magical mystery coach tour. You paid your money, and you never realised really where you were going to end up, but it seemed to be always the same. You'd go to the coach park, get in the coach, scenic route, you'd end up in a pub, the kids would be outside. We'd have a soft drink, a bag of crisps and my mum and dad would have a beer. Great days. Great walking, great fresh air and we were fortunate.

There weren't many in our street who actually went away for holidays. Still, amongst my friends, several of them went back to Ireland, Southern Ireland, to see their family.

We felt privileged actually, in a kind of way, it was an amazing feeling. I say to people now, the excitement and the anticipation of going away to Ramsgate and that Thanet coastline for two weeks matched anything that I've seen from my grandchildren. Even when we go to Florida, whilst they're excited it's not the same degree of excitement.

And still on the subject of holidays and the importance of holidays, I was Sales Director for Sandel Perkins, and in the mid-80s I was lucky to recruit from the competition a guy called Colin Pocock. Colin was a popular and experienced Sales Representative, a local lad to the Ashford area and very successful.

A good guy, nice guy, met his wife on several occasions at social events. Very shy, very nervous and he explained to me later that she'd been like that unfortunately since they lost their daughter at the age of fourteen. They did have a son as well, so there was one child in the family. And we spoke about holidays, because I said, "oh, you're not far, Ashford", telling him about my days in Ramsgate, Margate, Broadstairs and he told me that his parents, both his parents were deaf and dumb so their earnings were very meagre.

It must have been a tough life for him, and they used to go away once a year, and it meant so much to him. Their going away was getting a train from Ashford to Margate and spending the day on the coast. He said his mum would make sandwiches, they'd pick the day obviously in advance. Being a kid, he'd take a bucket and spade with him, and so would his sister. They'd leave early in the morning and spend the day on the beach and come home, and they would do that every year, one day a year. And holidays were particularly important to him, he was always one for looking for exciting venues and destinations for him and his wife and son. Colin later in the '80s emigrated to Canada.

You know we talk about breaks now, but anticipation is anticipation be it two weeks in Florida or be it one day in Margate once a year, the buzz and the sense of excitement was the same.

But really enjoyable, enjoyable times, summer holidays and as I said being street kids to a vast degree, much more so than in these days.

My mum worked in the market, as I mentioned previously, Queen's Crescent Market. She was known as Josie, Josie Elliott, to her family she was known as Fifi, her name was Josephina. The English called her Josie, the Italians called her Fifi. She was very popular, because to a lot of market traders Saturday night was a big night, and they would bring their suits into Mum and pick 'em up Saturday morning for their events Saturday night.

One evening, it was about half-past six, there was a knock on the door, which was unusual in our household apart from friends calling for us during the day, and my dad answered it, he said: "Josie, somebody here wants to speak to you". And there was one of the market traders, very apologetic, and explaining that he never had time to pick up his suit and would it be possible for Mum to go back to the Dry Cleaners, open up and give him his suit. My dad was against the idea, he thought it was a liberty to expect that to happen, but my mum being my mum, soft as anything, she walked back with the guy to Perkins Dry Cleaners, Queen's Crescent, opened up, turned the alarm off, gave him his suit. And on the Monday she was presented with a big box of chocolates. But that was my mum, she was very aware of other people, particularly her children.

I can remember now during our summer holidays, playing in the street, football, lunchtime we could see the figure of my mum walking very fast. She used to come home from work, it'd only be a ten-minute walk, walking fast, she'd come home, cook us a meal and then go back to work. Or if my brother and sister were doing something separately I would go to her Dry Cleaners at

Queen's Crescent, there's a little kitchenette in the back, and she would make me steak sandwiches. I'll always remember that I'd walk around listening to the market traders. They were very good times, very enjoyable, as was that period of time, I was now thirteen, and a Second year at school.

CHAPTER 17

ENTER GREAVES

Summer holidays over and a new exciting season for Spurs, Season '61-62, what could we hope for. We'd achieved the impossible dream of the Double in the previous season, could we actually get the Treble? The reason why the Treble was now a possibility was that Spurs would be in the European League Cup, the number one premier contest consisting of all the teams in Europe who'd reached number one position in their league, the equivalent to today's European Championship. The European Cup was seen by everybody as an almost impossible goal, only Manchester United reached the semi-final, most teams wouldn't even bother entering the contest, but United broke that mould. It was Spurs' opportunity now to prove, not only were they the best in Britain, possibly in the UK but they were the best in Europe.

So we were looking forward to an exciting season. Let's start off with the League, how did we fare in the League? Not quite the start we had in the previous season, but we were scoring goals, plenty of goals. To me the biggest event of that season was signing Jimmy Greaves, the great Jimmy Greaves, recognised in his era as the greatest goal scorer produced in England, he was just superb.

Jimmy Greaves was a cockney lad, 5ft 8", a child prodigy on the football field in the '50s, every scout of a top club was after signing Jimmy Greaves. He was scoring at will for local club sides and also county sides. Everybody was aware of Jimmy Greaves, from the age of fourteen he was there on the record book.

He was actually a Spurs supporter, but his father advised him against Spurs as they were known then as a buying club, probably more so than bringing them up through the youth. In the end, he settled for Chelsea, and there he made a name for himself.

In no time at all, he was in their first team as a teenager, scoring goals. On his debut for their first team, in the First Division, his debut was actually against Spurs. In that match Spurs were 1-0 ahead, towards the end Greaves got the ball, despite his youth and lack of experience he had the skill and the tenacity to beat three Spurs defenders, then go around the goalkeeper to score the equalising goal. Danny Blanchflower, after when he was asked to make a comment, said "this man is some player, and he will be a legend", and as normal, Danny Blanchflower was correct. Jimmy Greaves was a goal-scoring legend and still is.

He went on for another couple of seasons with Chelsea, played for England when he was under 20, scored in his debut and was regularly notching up as many as five goals for Chelsea. In one memorable match against the League champions, Wolverhampton Wanderers, it ended up 5-5, and Greaves scored all of Chelsea's 5 goals, an amazing player. Chelsea couldn't hold on to him, Milan I believe, either Inter or AC Milan, purchased him, bought him from Chelsea for a not-insignificant amount of money and played him in the Italian League.

But Greaves was unhappy, he was homesick. Despite being their top goal-scorer, he didn't last a year before he asked for a transfer. Bill Nicholson went straight to Italy, spoke to their directors and in no time at all had made an acceptable offer. It was £100,000 bar £1, Nicholson wanted to keep it below the hundred thousand mark. Jimmy Greaves was going back to England, but even more important, he was going back to Spurs. The fans were over the moon at having Greavesy back in England, but particularly the Spurs fans. Such a great goal-scorer, difficult to compare to anybody, I would say probably a combination of Lionel Messe and Robbie Fowler at his best. He was a goal-scorer of distinction, and he made his debut, and I was there, White Hart, a home debut at White Hart Lane.

His first match was in the reserves as was customary in those days, but his first formal match was in December, late December at White Hart Lane, and we were entertaining Blackpool. I was right on the front behind the Blackpool goal when Jimmy Greaves scored a hat-trick on his debut, and one of them was a scissors kick which was quite new and something he'd picked up from the continent. Three goals in his first game and that was in December.

Now in that season that we're talking about, '61-62, Jimmy Greaves played twenty-two First Division games for Spurs, and in those twenty-two, he scored 21 goals, an average of almost a goal a game which was unheard of. He was a great player; the crowd took to him straight away. But he had everything, probably not so good in the air he wasn't a big man, but could dribble to beat his man, had a good shot, he just used to pass it into the net. He had the ability to go around players, and he had fun, he was always with a smile on his face, and he was obviously enjoying his life at Spurs.

But despite Greaves, his contribution to the team, we failed in winning the League Championship in '62. It was a strange quirk really because the team who were the winners of the '62 League Championship had just come up from the second Division, Ipswich Town. You could have got 100-1 on Ipswich Town at the beginning of the season, they were managed by an ex-Spurs player who became a legend as the greatest England manager ever, Alf Ramsey.

Most of his career was at Tottenham where he played as a full-back alongside Bill Nicholson who was also at Spurs as a full-back and also played for England. He got his first taste of management at Ipswich Town. He introduced a new style of football which depended, more possibly on the 'long ball' than it did on the 'push and run' style, and one-touch style at Spurs. He had two big forwards up front, he had a really good defence. He focused very much on his defence, and Ipswich Town's tactics were different to anybody else in that season '62 and ended up champions. Spurs ended up in third place, which was no mean achievement, but ironically if Spurs hadn't lost to Ipswich Town at home, Spurs would have been the champions. Well, that's football for you.

The last team to be promoted and in their first season in the First Division to win the Championship was actually Spurs in 1951 with their famous push and run theme, they gained promotion, and they won the League title. So Spurs finished in third place, beaten to it really by their defeat at home to Ipswich, but we were third. That left the Cup, and the Cup was always important to the fans, the FA Cup was still the premier trophy of the season, and the European Cup.

CHAPTER 18

CUP GLORY

So Spurs were in search of regaining the FA Cup in 1962. I was there for all their home matches. They started off with an away fixture to Birmingham, and thanks to 2 goals by Jimmy Greaves we managed to hang on to a 3-3 draw and play Birmingham at home on the following Wednesday.

We won that match 4-2, thanks to goals again, 1 goal by Greaves, 1 goal by Allen, who'd replaced Bobby Smith, and 2 goals by Terry Medwin, who was unfortunate not to be in Spurs first team, he was ousted by Terry Dyson. Medwin was a very skilful welsh international, very good in the air, very good crosser of the ball, in another team he'd have been a regular player.

Our next game was away to a Third Division team, Plymouth Argyle, and we thrashed them 5-1. Greaves again scored two goals. Then we played West Bromwich Albion, a strong team, in the February away from home, we beat them 4-2, Jimmy Greaves, once again scored two goals.

And then the big one, home to Aston Villa, one of the top teams, White Hart Lane, great atmosphere. It was a cup match, and once again ticket touts everywhere, all the shop fronts displaying their signs, 'Spurs first for the

Double FA Cup'. There was a sense of excitement and achievement and Spurs were up for it, and we beat them 2-0, thanks to goals by Blanchflower and Jones. In the '62 Cup run that was the only game that Greaves failed to score.

The next game, which was against Manchester United, was the semi-final. A big team United, a big team even then, just before the Best era but they had the likes of Law, Charlton, Stiles, Paddy Crerand, it was a good, good strong team managed by the number one, Busby, and we beat them 3-1.

That game was played at Hillsborough in Sheffield, with the goals by Medwin again, Greaves and Jones, then it was the Final, could we do it? We'd slipped up in the League, but we had the Cup Final, and again I was quite happy watching that on television. One has to bear in mind once again that watching live football on television in the early '60s was so unusual it was a once in a year experience. Internationals, as I mentioned before, were shown live, but football, cup football, league football wasn't. The Cup Final was the only other game shown live and it was a big event.

So once again Spurs were in there as holders, and they were determined to put on a much better show. Despite winning the previous year against Leicester's ten men they were not at their peak, but this time Spurs turned it on against Burnley. In a really exciting game Spurs took the lead, Burnley equalised, Spurs scored two more goals.

Goal-scorers, once again, Jimmy Greaves; Bobby Smith; Danny Blanchflower from the penalty spot. Spurs had done what no other team had ever done, they regained the Cup in the following season, and they played with style and flair, and they were once again the toast of the town.

CHAPTER 19

FOILED BY BENFICA

I did mention that there were three trophies up that season, and of course for the first time ever, in season '62 due to their success in the previous year winning the League Spurs were in the European Cup, which we now call the Champions League. Spurs were unknown in Europe, never competed there before, totally unknown but recognised to be a force by those who knew their football. It nearly ended up in disaster, their very first match Spurs played the Polish champions, Górnik Zabrze, and they went in there as the Double winners against the Polish champions.

Now can you believe it, first leg, a two-legged affair, we're playing Górnik in Poland, a draw would be handy because we'd then get the replay at Spurs, a victory would be great. With twenty minutes to go, Tottenham were 4-0 down, it looked like disaster. For all the debate about the greats at White Hart Lane, what a tremendous team they were, were they to fail when pitted against European competition, were we that far behind the best team in Poland? No we weren't because in the closing minutes Spurs scored two goals. They still lost 4-2 but the second leg was to come at White Hart Lane and White Hart Lane was buzzing that evening. It was the first European game the fans had witnessed.

Spurs played all in white and desperate to make up for their embarrassing first leg performance. On that night was born the tradition of Spurs in European glory, of the fans singing, of the expectation, it was an amazing atmosphere. I was there, I was fortunate enough to be there. I went by myself, one of my dad's pals managed to get me a ticket, and it was a tremendous atmosphere. Spurs came out winners 8-1 against the Polish champions in front of a crowd of 56,770. Goal scorers were Jones 3, Smith 2, Blanchflower, Jones and Dyson 1 each. Now bear in mind scarcely ten days before, at one stage Spurs were 4-0 down - so they had scored 10 goals against 1 goal after that initial scare.

As I went home, the fans were singing, the air was full of joy, happiness. I got home late that night but still made school the following morning, so all was well, but I was told that I couldn't repeat that performance when I got home so late. I didn't care I was there, I was there for one of the biggest games in Spurs history, their first venture into Europe, facing a difficult task losing the first leg 4-2, and they thrashed them 8-1, what a game.

We went on in that season, Spurs, we played lots of top clubs from Europe, and we got as far as the semi-finals. The only other team to make the semi-finals was Manchester United in the past. We were there, we were facing Benfica over two legs. Benfica were the kings of Portugal. They had a great squad of players, Portuguese internationals, and amongst them the world-class Eusébio, who was one of the top goal scorers of the '60s. Spurs lost the first game which meant that in their second game, at White Hart Lane, that they had to win by a clear two-goal margin, unfortunately, they won by a one-goal margin.

There was a lot of debate about several goals that Spurs had scored and were ruled offside when they felt clearly that they were not. There was a lot of bitterness, there was a lot of sadness because they felt they were hard done by, but at the end of the day, Benfica was an amazingly good team. Spurs lost to a good team, and we were now out of the European Cup, but we had played admirably and had proven our value to other teams in Europe. We were one of the best teams in Europe, but at the final hurdle, we didn't make it. So, to me, it was still a great season. We finished third in the League due to one result at White Hart Lane. We won the FA Cup in style, and we got to the semi-final of the top competition in Europe. And most importantly we had Jimmy Greaves in our side.

CHAPTER 20

CASUAL WORK

Season '62-63 proved to be another very successful season for Spurs, the highest goal scoring Spurs team. Before we go on to the next chapter of the football saga, socially things were changing a lot, particularly 1963. I was approaching fifteen, I was in the third year, getting on for the fourth year at school and things were changing dramatically in the '60s.

I would say the major change we would see would obviously be on music. I'd heard a fair bit of music as my sister being four years older and having a gramophone she used to play a lot, and obviously hearing it on the radio as well. But, we suddenly went from the days of Helen Shapiro, Billy Fury, Tommy Steele, Cliff Richards, mainly solo singers, with possibly some of them with backing bands. I guess there were about a dozen well-known pop stars, as we called them, popular singers around at that time.

Most of the music people thrived on was from America, and that would be an assortment of black artists and solo white singers. But all of a sudden the Beatles came on to the scene and things changed forever. The Merseybeat it was called because soon after the Beatles made their entrance, they were followed up with people also from

Liverpool, like the Merseybeats, Freddy and the Dreamers, the Searchers, Gerry and the Pacemakers, it seemed that every week there was a new band. Liverpool led, Manchester and London followed soon after. I know as I guess a fully-fledged teenager now, I and my pals who I hung around with, we were aware of the sort of social change.

I remember us copying the Beatles and getting our first Cuban heel boots, that was the rage Cuban heel boots, I wasn't into flairs at that time, and Beatle hairstyles weren't a big thing but Cuban heel boots I certainly wore. I grew up in that period where, as a male of that age, you were judged on I suppose strange features compared to today, or maybe not. Firstly - if you wanted to be seen as being a top man, you were hard. By hard, I mean being considered a good fighter (even if you weren't) as most people went on recognition, perception rather than action. And I was probably one of those, only because in my junior school I had a couple of fights and came out okay. But, technically it was all about junior school, and the first year in senior school I had a tag of maybe Elliott was a little bit hard. In fact, I was anything but, but I'm not going to turn it away.

Secondly, on the factor, the X-factor would be clothes. Suddenly people were aware of clothes, fourteen, fifteen you were expected to wear a certain standard. Gone were the days when you used to go out at night in your school uniform, or weekend in your school uniform. I never did, but quite a few in my school did. You'd see them weekends still in their school uniform, and that was really uncool, you would change straightaway.

Unlike today there were few important brand names with the exception of Levi jeans, you would purchase crew neck jumpers from M & S and suits from Burtons or John Colliers (the window to watch) It was an ambition to be seen as being a good cool dresser. You'd supplement your meagre pocket money with now at the age of fourteen meaning you could work, you could have part-time work, Saturday work.

I had a host of jobs over that time from fourteen to fifteen until I eventually went to work at sixteen. I was a paperboy; I was a packer at Tescos in Kentish Town. Supermarkets were still relatively new, not used a lot by our family because of my mother's ability to do her shopping at the market. But a lot of people were using supermarkets, and each till would have a packer, and I was one of those packers. You'd stand at the end of the till and as the food was going through it was your job to pack them into carrier bags for the customer, I quite enjoyed that.

I also managed through my brother, to get a weekend job at London Zoo on the catering side. Even at the relatively young age of thirteen or fourteen 'looking good' was imperative and therefore weekend and holiday work to raise cash was crucial. My big brother Peter had been working at the London Zoo for several years. He was well established and suggested I turn up at the main entrance of London Zoo at 8.00 am and line up with those seeking casual work.

It was a strange situation there, you would go to the Zoo early, you would line up, and the catering managers would come along. There would be four different departments for catering, and they would pick who they wanted to work that day. Obviously, if they had a record of you working for them previously and they knew of you, you would be selected, and some would be told automatically to go in the next day and would carry on working. But there was always a queue of young lads standing there, and I caught the eye of Lionel, who was in charge of one of the restaurants. Or should I say Lionel caught my eye as he walked past me with a strange duck walk, black dyed hair combed back and a hint of make-up on his face. And he said I'll have him and he picked me out, and I worked the day for Lionel. I remember coming home telling my brother I'd been successful, he said "who are you working for?", I said Lionel, he said "God, not Lionel", he said "do not turn your back on him", and they were the last words on the topic. But, any way I got on well with Lionel, he was a nice lad, so I had that going for me.

I also managed to get a job at Leadstones the Butchers in Hampstead High Street, and I was a delivery boy. Quite daunting at first out on a pushbike with a basket, I'd had a bike by then so I did know how to cycle.

Cycling around the streets of Hampstead, knocking on doors and delivering their meat which was packed up in greaseproof paper with a pin and a name and address. Occasionally I'd get a couple of pennies tip or sometimes even a sixpenny bit. And what was really nice was that at the end of the day, Leadstones the Butcher's manager would make me up a little parcel. Might have a couple of chops in there and maybe even a bit of steak, a few sausages. He would say to me, "Elliott, take that home to Mum", and I'd take my parcel back.

I also later got a job in Burtons in Camden Town High Street, and that was vital because as I approached sixteen, my fifth year at school, I was going out socially more. It was the style to have a suit and Burtons and Colliers were the people to go to, you could get a 'made to measure' suit there for £12. If you were working on a Saturday, which was probably £1 wages, you could save up, and you could get a suit made. And because I worked at Burtons I got it at staff price, either off the peg or made. It seems strange now that school kids were getting suits made in the '60s, but clothes were such an important part.

So it was clothes, a perception of being hard, and there were your contacts. Did your brother belong to a local gang? Were you friends with some real toughies? Who did you know? It's quite tangled, but it did score brownie points. My brother wasn't a member of any gang, his life was devoted to animals, he had very good friends, and they all worked in the Zoo, so they were a separate sect. A couple of my friends had older brothers who were in the infamous Somer's Town crew, so they got bonus points. If people picked on them "do you know who his brother is? Murphy, Murphy, yeah Murphy, knocks about with the Somer's Town Crew", "Jesus, Jesus, no sorry about that, forget it."

So that was good, and the other big thing that had changed is that suddenly girls seemed to be a major attraction, hence the need to look smart and dress smart. But it was good, I wasn't aware of a big increase in crime or even in drugs. I think I've already mentioned my friend, really close friend Brian O'Sullivan who was ahead of his time, unfortunately died in his very early twenties through a drug overdose. But the only drugs that we saw or heard about were Black Bombers, and they were pretty mild compared to today. They were more of an energy boost, but I wasn't aware of any really hard drugs, certainly nobody I knew. I guess there was smoking and that certainly wasn't Pot. You could buy cigarettes loose as well, there were certain shops where you could go in and for tuppence, I think, could buy a cigarette. I remember going into a cinema on a Sunday afternoon and trying to look the part, we might buy a packet of twenty American cigarettes and stick 'um in your pocket. But they'd last you for months, it was all 'show off'.

CHAPTER 21

THE GREAT ESCAPE

Crime, amongst people I knew, I guess the major one was doing the meter, which meant going into somebodies house, into their basement and breaking into their gas meter. A lot of houses didn't lock their doors because parents were working, and children who were on holiday from school needed access. Obviously, I never got involved in that. And also telephone boxes, it seems so minor now for what the rewards were, a screwdriver opening a telephone box and taking the coins. Bearing in mind it was 12 pennies to the shilling, 240 pennies to the pound, and those boxes could only take pennies, so if you managed to get away with a few pounds, you'd be weighed down. Two of my pals were caught doing that and had to go to court, and got severely reprimanded for stealing from the phone box.

It was fairly crime-free, mugging wasn't around then. Unfortunately, with the older boys, there was queer-bashing on Hampstead Heath which was something we were aware of. Groups of guys would go out and look for solitary men, they'd presume they maybe gay and sort of threaten them and take their money. We heard about that, but there wasn't really much crime, you could walk the streets and even go into other territories as long as you did it with a bit of care and attention.

I guess the nearest I got to big trouble in my teens was one Christmas Eve when my parents had bought me, through a book club, a suede duffel coat, my pride and joy. They gave me permission to wear it, I was going to a friend's family party in Somers Town. I didn't leave there until gone midnight, and I walked, it wasn't a long walk down Hampstead Road, from Somers Town to Camden Town. At that stage, we were living in Camden, not Kentish Town. I was suddenly aware that across the road two guys, nobody else around. I recognised one of the faces, they were both three or four years older than me. And the one I recognised was from the infamous Somers Town Crew, and they were after obviously, my beloved suede coat. A difficult situation, I knew I'd have to make a run for it. They were looking at me now from the other side of the road chatting to each other, and on the count of three, I just bolted. They bolted after me shouting out obscenities warning me that if they got hold of me they'd give me a good kicking, but drop my coat and they'd leave me. I just kept on going no way was I going to release my coat. We ran all the way down Camden High Street to Camden Tube Station, I turned right going towards Caledonian Road, they chased after me. It went on for about twenty minutes, I always managed to keep at least twenty yards away from the two of them, and in the end, they just gave up, I didn't, I kept on running. I was living in a place called Agar Grove and got home, mass of sweat, took my coat off and thought thank Christ I've still got it. I wake up, and it's Christmas Day.

CHAPTER 22

'62/63

But now let's focus on the football. '62-63 would prove to be another extremely exciting season for Spurs. Once again, they could potentially do the Treble, which had never been done before as with the Double previously. The reason why was that Spurs were the favourites to win the League after finishing third in the previous year, and favourites to retain the FA Cup. Spurs were the holders of the FA Cup because they had won it '61-62. And once again Spurs were in Europe. Not in the premier competition which was the European Cup, but by virtue of beating Burnley in the Cup Final, they were in the Europeans Cup Winners Cup. A competition that was the second most prized European competition, open to all the European teams that had won their respective Cup Finals, so there were some very, very good teams in there.

So potentially the Treble was up for Spurs once again, and they had a good squad of players. They had the backbone of the Double team plus the one and only Jimmy Greaves. They'd had Jimmy Greaves for a full season and bearing in mind the previous season he'd scored 30 goals in 29 league and cup games, what was he capable of in a full season, 40+ most pundits thought. So it was kick-off time, and Spurs started the season with a good victory beating Birmingham City 3-0 at home. Unfortunately, that was followed by a loss away. It was a bit of a strange season for Spurs, I mean they played well, I went to most matches. Exciting football but I guess the most notable factor of that particular season was the number of goals Spurs scored. They were in excellent goal-scoring form, once again they scored over 100 goals in the League, and Jimmy Greaves was the outstanding player. In the League in '62-63, he scored 37 goals. And that particular season, the highlight I guess, one of many highlights, was Spurs scoring 111 goals in the League that season. They were regularly putting three, four or more goals past the competition.

I will highlight some of the high scoring games. West Ham away, Spurs have always been their fiercest opponent. Spurs beat them at West Ham 6-1, Greaves 2 goals. The biggy home to Nottingham Forest, I can still remember that game for the quality of the goals that were scored. Nottingham Forest was a good team, in the top half of the table. In front of a crowd of 50,000 Spurs beat them 9-2, Greaves, the invincible Greaves scored 4 goals. The famous Sam Leitch writing in the *Sunday Pictorial* (September 30th 1962) headlines read 'A Carve-Up Spurs' followed by 'Greaves Leads Slaughter'. The amazing stat from that game was that Forest scored first after five minutes and five minutes later Spurs were winning 2-1 thanks to 2 goals by Greaves, and Forest scored last but, unfortunately for Forest, Spurs scored 9 goals in between!

Then the following match we played Arsenal and drew 4-4. Then a couple of matches later, home against Manchester United, who we'd beaten in the previous year in the semi-final. Again United a very strong team and getting stronger with Law, Charlton, Stiles, and Stepney in goal it was a great team. We played them at White Hart Lane, and we beat them 6-2, Jimmy Greaves with a hat-trick, what a player. One of his goals often shown on television, goal-scoring highlights of the past, he dribbles past four United defenders and then past the goalkeeper, what a game, it was brilliant to be there. The next game after that 6-2 thrashing was away to Leyton Orient who'd been newly promoted, 5-1 they were beaten. The next real high scoring game, we'd had quite a few fours and threes against Ipswich Town who we beat 5-0 with yet another hat-trick from Greaves. Now, by the way, we'd first played Ipswich Town in the first game of the season, a traditional game of The Charity Shield, where the winners of League played the winners of the Cup. It gave Tottenham a chance to prove they were a better team than Ipswich, and this was played at Wembley and Spurs beat Ipswich 5-1.

Ipswich were a one-season wonder, they finished quite low down that season, and the following season they were relegated, but without their manager Alf Ramsey. Alf Ramsey was rewarded for his success at Ipswich by becoming the manager of England and led them to the 1966 World Cup Final. The next real big high scoring match for Spurs was Liverpool. Liverpool were newly promoted and a very strong team under the guidance of supremo Bill Shankley. They had many internationals, great goal scorers such as Hunt, Thompson, and Ian St John, but when they played Spurs at White Hart Lane Spurs beat them 7-2 in front of 54,000. And once again Greaves scored 4 goals, what a great goal scorer he was. And once again Greaves scored 4 goals, what a great goal scorer he was. So at the end of the season, Jimmy Greaves in 41 games had scored 37 goals, almost a goal a game and a repeat of the previous season. Amazing, if you include the previous season's goals he'd already got close to a 100 goals in League and Cup matches after being at the club for just under two seasons, including his goals in Europe which we'll talk about later.

Now our final position in the League was second, having missed the Championship by a couple of points. Still, it was a great, great season for Spurs, a great goal scoring season. Not only was Jimmy Greaves in the goals also in the goals was Cliff Jones. When you think he was a winger - he scored 20 goals.

Cliff Jones was a tremendous player for Spurs and will always feature amongst the world-class players who graced White Hart Lane. At 5ft 7" he was fast, skilful and brave, when he signed for Spurs in 1958 from Swansea for £35,000 it was a club record but what a great player. Jones finished at Spurs in '68/69 season with 370 appearances and 159 goals, an all-time great. Dave Mackay scored

6 goals, and for a centre-back, that was quite a score. Bobby Smith wasn't playing so much; it was Smith playing or Allen. Bobby Smith was still probably number one, Les Allen number two, both of them behind Greaves. John White, Scottish international midfielder, who was soon to die in tragic circumstances when he was struck by lightning playing golf, scored 8 goals. But in all, including own goals, Spurs scored 111 goals.

So we got close to the Championship, but we were second. In the FA Cup, bearing in mind we'd beaten Burnley the previous year, Leicester City the year before that, our first round was home to Burnley, and I think most people would have tipped Spurs to come away with their name still in the hat. But it wasn't to be. I remember the disappointment amongst the crowd who were hoping we could get the Treble off a Cup Final win. But we lost at home in front of a reasonably large crowd, and we lost at home to Burnley 3-0. I think it was one of the few occasions that season, only happened three times in the League when we failed to score, and we were beaten 3-0. For the supporters that was a pretty sad dismal day, any idea of the Treble was gone. Still, we made a really good show in the League to finish second.

CHAPTER 23

EUROPE AND GLORY

So what else could we achieve this season? We were in the Cup Winners Cup, as I mentioned earlier, and that was a prestigious competition. One must remember no British club had ever won a European Competition in the history of European matches, so this was the new adventure for Spurs. Obviously, they were in a stronger position because they weren't playing the teams that had won their League, they were playing the teams that had managed to secure their countries Cup. It was very big in England, it was big in most countries, FA Cup, Spanish Cup, Portuguese, it was high profile, particularly so in England. So, what would fate have in store for us in the European Cup Winners Cup? Well, the first match was very interesting, a two-legged affair which pitted us in the October against Glasgow Rangers.

Now Glasgow Rangers were the undisputed champions of Scotland, and they had a team packed with Scottish internationals. It was the first time, I believe in a competitive match, that a top English club had played a top Scottish club, and the first leg was to be held at White Hart Lane. There was a crowd of 60,000 and Spurs came out victorious 5-2. It was very dubious whether Glasgow Rangers could turn that around, they'd have to win by 4 clear goals, and the next round Spurs won 3-2, which gave us an aggregate win of 8-4. Greaves was again a goal scorer, and when I look at that team, and I have the evidence of the Spurs team in front of me, what a strong team it was. Bill Brown Scottish international in goal; Baker, a home-grown lad, full-back; Henry, soon to play for England, home-grown full-back; Danny Blanchflower, captain of Ireland, Footballer of the Year, tremendous player; Morris Norman, regular England centre-half, strong in the tackle, great in the air; and the one and only Davy Mackay, who also captained Scotland, ferocious mid-fielder with all the skills one could ask for.

Because we had an injury to both Dyson and Medlin we had a local lad on one of the flanks, Frank Saul, Canvey Island lad, again Spurs youth, who ended up with a good career at Spurs. Next to him was John White, the ghost of White Hart Lane, the way he could slot into position, a great provider and a good goal scorer. We also had Bobby Smith, whilst close to the end of his days at Spurs was still banging in the goals, and alongside him the one and only Jimmy Greaves, and Cliff Jones who was scoring 20 goals a season for Spurs out on the flanks, great player, a great team. So we actually beat them 8-4 on aggregate.

The next leg pitted us against a team from Bratislava, one of the eastern European teams who were champions of their own League. The first leg was away, and we lost 2-0, and that was difficult, next we then had to play them at White Hart Lane. Now to lose 2-0 in an away competition and not score meant you had to beat the other team by at least 3 goals, and they were a tough, hard team. We met them at White Hart Lane and beat them 6-0. Goal scorers were White, Smith, Greaves 2, and Jones and MacKay.

We were now in the semi-finals, drawn against OFK Belgrade, over the two legs we beat them 5-2 and were now in the final against a really top European team. The final was held in Rotterdam in Holland. The other team in question was a famous Madrid team, not Real Madrid but Atlético Madrid who were a tremendous team in Spain packed with Spanish internationals. Tottenham's confidence, unfortunately, suffered a blow with an injury to their key man before the game, Dave Mackay.

Now Dave MacKay was the heart of the Spurs team, Blanchflower was the soul, and Greaves was the finisher. MacKay was full of confidence, he could lead players to believe in themselves, his energy and confidence lifted everybody at White Hart Lane. He lifted the fans, he lifted the players, demoralised the opposition. So as Spurs sat in the final, in the changing room, 40,000 crowd equally divided between English and Spanish fans, Bill Nicholson spoke to the team and obviously went through the opposing players.

Danny Blanchflower in his biography gives us a good idea and feel of the moment as Nicholson bemoaning a lack of MacKay went through Atlético Madrid, highlighting the skills and the experience and the energy of their players. Suddenly Danny Blanchflower got up and said: "hold on

Bill, I appreciate what you're saying, they are a good team, but let's be fair we haven't got Dave MacKay, but we've got a bloody good substitute in Tony Marchi".

Now, Tony Marchi had played for Spurs in the late '50s, Edmonton boy, Italian background as his name would suggest, excellent half-back. He was signed by Juventus and spent several seasons in Italy and had come back to Spurs in 1960, he was a very capable player and at one time had been captain of Spurs. And Blanchflower pointed out, "look at us Bill, look what we've achieved in the last few seasons, look at our team. Is there a better forward than Jimmy Greaves? Is there a better wide player than Cliff Jones? Is there a better goalkeeper than Bill Brown? Is there a stronger centre-half than Morris Norman? Is there a more skilful inside forward than John White?" And he went on and went on and went through every Spurs player. In the end, they were full of confidence, bursting to get out there, and when they did, they played tremendously. They were in superb form, they were a credit to Spurs, they were a credit to England.

They thrashed Atlético Madrid 5-1, and it was a thrashing, it could have been 7-1 or 8-1. Spurs again all in white, had won a European trophy. They paraded around the ground holding the trophy high, Spurs fans cheering them on, the whole of England cheering them on, the whole of Britain hopefully cheering them on. This was a British side who'd come to Europe and conquered and one that everyone should feel proud of.

Spurs hadn't achieved the Treble, and it would be one day as we all know, almost 40 years later accomplished by Manchester United. Whilst we hadn't won the Treble, we'd come second runners up in the League, and we failed dismally in the FA Cup, unfortunately. Still, we had won the European Cup Winners Cup. And Jimmy Greaves once again shone, he'd scored his 37 goals in the League, he also scored 6 goals in Europe giving him a total for the season of 43 goals. Amazing return, amazing success, so another as far as the supporters were concerned, and the press, another great season for the Lily Whites.

MADRID MAULED 5-1

Super Spurs won the European Cup Winner's Cup tonight with a five-goal massacre of Madrid and became the first British Club to carry off one of Europe's top Soccer trophies, it was in the tradition of true champions that Spurs wrote another glorious chapter in their history.

Goal scorers – Greaves (16', 78')

Dyson (69', 87')

White (32')

EXTRACT FROM THE *DAILY MIRROR* MAY 16th 1962, KEN JONES (ROTTERDAM)

CHAPTER 24

NOBLE ART

Whilst, as I've already mentioned '63-64 saw great social change in Britain, in my household actually, there wasn't a lot of change, it took a few years for it to come. Routines were very similar, particularly weekends, which would either be me playing football or calling for my pal Terry O'Leary and going shopping at Queens Crescent Market.

One notable incident happened to us, I remember we were about twelve. In Terry's road, a family of Jamaicans had come over for a family funeral and decided to stay in the UK, and they were renting a house. There was a son who was our age and two young sisters who would have been about eight or nine with the old traditional pigtails that the West Indian girls had. Being the ignorant lads we were, we were taking the mickey out of the girls, and their brother appeared. We already knew his name was Basil, so we started calling him 'Basil the Brush, boom, boom' more like bang, bang, he hit us both. He didn't floor us but stunned us enough to make a hasty retreat and never tangle with Basil again.

Basil actually became a boxer and boxed in the St Pancras Gym under a famous trainer and his boxing title was Bunny Sterling. He got the British Championship, beat Mark Rowe, an Eastend lad. He also secured the

European Championship middle-weight in 1976. One of the finest middle-weights produced in Britain, the first Caribbean immigrant to win a British title. Just goes to show you, be careful who you pick on.

Actually, a sad ending to that, not particularly with him, but with his manager. We knew his manager, he was the local Camden Town boy, George Francis, he was a keen athlete and also an ex-boxer. One of my pals, Terry Francis, was his nephew, and we worked together at Elliot Perkins. He was a well-respected man George Francis, Terry's uncle, he was one of the first trainers to actually give black youngsters a chance. He really focused on the black youth of Camden and on that area as he could see the talent and the ability to become great boxers. Prior to that, they were ignored to a certain amount, they weren't seen as being box office value because of the colour of their skin. But he didn't take any notice of that, and he treated them like one big family.

Not only did he have Bunny Sterling he also had some involvement in progressing Frank Bruno to the World Championship, and I guess his greatest prodigy was John Conteh who was World Champion for a number of years, a scouser. We used to often see John Conteh, he used to train with Francis in Hampstead Heath. They'd be running around the park, and we as kids would run behind.

George Francis was recognised as one of the great Boxing Trainers of his generation. He started his career as a bare-knuckle fighter in the slums of North London in the 1930s and went on to mentor many World, European and British champions. Very much a family man, but suffered several cruel blows through the years with the death of his wife and son through cancer, and then his son-in-law being killed in a car crash in South Africa. Sadly, fighting depression, George Francis took his own life in 2002 aged 73. A real unhappy ending for a man who did a lot to inspire black youngsters, particularly in London, giving them a chance to box and make a name for themselves and there was a hell of a lot of respect for him.

CHAPTER 25

FAMILY TRADITIONS

Anyway, back to our routine. So I was playing football; Saturday afternoon still tended to be one of watching the telly with my dad, watching the wrestling; waiting for the football results, that's if I wasn't watching Spurs, and Sunday was probably the same in many households. For us kids, it was church in the morning, then my dad would insist on a long walk. We would start at Parliament Fields, all the way up into Hampstead Heath, up Hampstead Heath, Kenwood, Whitestone Pond, down again and home. Home for one o'clock, Sunday roast. Dad would go to sleep in the afternoon, we had to be quiet, if he was woken up, it wouldn't be very nice. It was a traditional seafood salad in the afternoon from the Seafood Man who came round the street. And Sunday night was bath night and London Palladium, and that seemed to go on forever for me.

There was a change, alternate Sundays, my mum and I, just my mum and I, would get a couple of buses to Wood Green to see her brother Carmeno and his wife Miluzza and the Piacentini family. There were six children, but quite often her other brothers and my uncles and aunties would be there so there would be about twenty in the household, all speaking Italian. I used to love it, just listening. I didn't understand what was being said, but the hand language and grimaces told me all I needed to know. And that was a traditional Sunday really, and it didn't change for many years.

I guess the following year football diminished. Whilst Spurs was always important to me I'd had my golden years in the 13-2 result; '61 Double; in the '62 FA Cup Final; the semi-final of a European Cup and in the '63 winning a European Trophy. I still went to Spurs, not as regularly, other things took over, studies, girlfriends, other things in life. But I look back through that time with a feeling of great love and affection for that period from 10-1 at halftime right through to the following three seasons.

CHAPTER 26

0-0 AT FULL TIME

Since that time Spurs have been involved in many epic matches. Up to this season 2020, Spurs have only been out of the top tier on one occasion when they got relegated in 1978. They bounced right back the following year so missed one year since 1951 when they were first promoted. They've only had one year in 70 outside of the top tier, the only clubs to equal that would be Arsenal and Everton. They've won numerous FA Cup Finals since, they've won the League Cup Finals, and they've won several more European contests. They've also reached the finals of the European Championship top European contest, and in 2019 loosing unfortunately to Liverpool. But for all their success, for all their innovations, for all the great players that had graced Spurs since that admirable Double's season when we won the League and the Cup, unfortunately, we have never won the League. So we have to go back 60 years to the last time a Spurs team won the League. We came close to it in the last four, five years, we've had a really good squad of players, second only to the Double team. But, unfortunately, when it came to the crunch finals and semi-finals, we were never quite there. So we live in hope, we've got our new stadium, we've got good financial backing, good youth team and loyal supporters.

I was forever drumming into my young lad Marc, 'glorious 10-1', 'glorious first season', my first match at Spurs, harping on about all that you've read over the last couple of hours. Obviously, Marc a Spurs supporter, he had no choice, but he is quite happy about that. At the age of seven, it was his seventh birthday actually. We went to White Hart Lane, it was 1977, to watch Spurs who were floundering a bit in that season. We had a home game against Middlesbrough, and it was his first match, on his birthday. Thoughts of 10-1 at halftime sprung to mind, but I was very dubious that we would get such a handsome victory. To make it even better for my lad was that, at the time I was a sales representative for Sandel Perkins and one of my customers, who I got on extremely well with, was Markheath Construction based in Whetstone, N20. And the buyer there, Geoffrey Springer, a very avid Spurs fan who, when I told him I was taking Marc to his first Spurs match, kindly offered me tickets. It was his boss's tickets who was on holiday, and he was taking care of them, there were two, two season tickets. I didn't realise until I got into the ground that Geoffrey's boss was a Director of Spurs, hence, Marc and I, for Marc's first match, sat in the Directors' Box. And the score at halftime was nil-nil, and the score at full-time was nil-nil. Spurs that particular season, 1977, were actually relegated into the Second Division. So for my son, it wasn't the glorious experience his dad had witnessed. But, over the years, there were many glorious experiences, and we still go to Spurs together now. Not as often as I used to, but my son, only two seasons ago, fulfilled one of his bucket wishes. He attended every single match home and away, and in Europe, that Spurs played in that particular season. It was season 2016, so it was a good season to watch Spurs.

But at the end of the day, you support your team, sometimes you're in luck, sometimes they're playing tremendous football. Unfortunately, there are times when they are losing, but your support never waivers, they will always be your team, be it nil-nil or 10-1 at halftime.

"COME ON YOU SPURS!"

ANTHONY AND HIS WIFE JEANETTE CELEBRATING THEIR
50TH WEDDING ANNIVERSARY
MARCH 2020

Printed in Great Britain
by Amazon

37951160R00069